AS I JOURNEY ALONG:

A Ghanaian's Perception Of Life In The Diaspora

Gabriel Baffour Awuah

To
Gabriela
And
Hanna

Contents

Preface

The more I wait with my accounts of the experiences I have gathered, ever since I set my foot in the Diaspora, the more I get bothered by the fact that I am missing something which is very important. What I am about to miss is the knowledge that I need to share with many people, before it becomes too late for me to do that. Those experiences can be of benefit to many people, the world over, especially those born and bred in the so called developing World. The experiences that I have made might not be unique in the sense that I might not be the only person that has those stories (about to be related and analysed later in this book) to tell. It is just that exactly the same stories have not yet been told by anyone.

My stories are rooted, for example, in the way I feel detached from my country of birth, the way I try to understand why things are as they are, seen from the experiences I have gathered from living in the Diaspora. The stories are also rooted in my encounters with my own country men and women that I have had contacts with in the Diaspora and in my motherland, Ghana. I also have stories about my encounters with other men and women from other countries in Africa, contacts with some other Africans occurred in the Diaspora. I have visited a number of countries in the Western World, where many Ghanaians in particular and Africans in general are living and working or studying. The interaction with many Africans, as I travel along, has enriched my stories about the plight of a Ghanaian, for example, in the Diaspora. Finally, I look through my stories and I try to discuss the concept of brain drain from a new perspective. I end my stories by offering some thoughts for deliberation.

I am grateful to have had contacts with many Ghanaians and some Africans in the various countries in the Diaspora that I have lived in or visited. They have all, in one way or the other, influenced my view of the world and the kind of understanding that I have today about the impact of the interactions between people. I express my gratitude to all that have come in my way to influence my view of the world, especially that of Ghana, that I now want to share with as many people as possible. I have no intention whatsoever to hurt anyone personally by narrating my stories, phrased under the heading "As I journey along". I would like to bring it home to all and sundry that I would be very sorry, if anyone would bring it to my notice that I have hurt him or her; because that is not the intention of my stories. I have to add that all accounts or stories given in this book are solely mine. I alone can be held responsible for the mistakes and/or the blunders that might be apparent to any reader.

1

Detached From My Country of Birth: Reflections Through The Diaspora Spectacle

Social Detachment

Having lived in the Diaspora for more than two decades, I feel very detached from my country of birth, Ghana. Every sector in the Ghanaian society has undergone some changes, socially, politically, economically and technologically, for example. The way people used to live in large family groups, grandparents, grandchildren, mothers and fathers, each of which have cousins all being part of the households is virtually vanishing. Small family households, comprising only parents and their own children, plus perhaps an aged parent (not the two parents of the couples) of one of the couples might luckily be living with the core family members depicted here. This reduction of the family size has come about as the result of many individuals who have had the opportunity to live and to work in the Diaspora (in the various parts of our rich world), acquiring thereby the financial ability to put up their own houses. Rarely would someone that has once lived in Europe, North America and any other place, other than Ghana, and has returned home with purchasing power to build own house or buy one, would want to live together with the extended family members. Of course, there are exceptions. Some may offer to live with one or two other people, mostly young ones who might be a nephew or niece to the 'returnee' from the Diaspora.

Even those 'well-to-do' that have never lived in the Diaspora are also prone to live in their houses with only the core family members, parent and children. Again, there are exceptions. One important trend that has emerged to compensate and/or satisfy some other family members, those excluded from the newly emerged trend (the core family), is for the 'partially detached' family member to build or help build additional house for the extended family members. The effect of this social change is that the majority of the people, which have not been outside Ghana to acquire some wealth, are not able to build houses just for their core family members. An important implication of this disparity is that it has become a trend to invest all efforts that would help one come to live in the Diaspora, for it is there that the chances to acquire wealth is the greatest, especially when one is aspired to have a house of his or her own.

What has not changed at all, is the lack of a national policy, on the part of succeeding governments, to provide and/or stimulate private businesses and co-operative organisations to enter the housing sector to help build numerous and affordable houses for the majority of the people. The general perception in the society is that most people, just living on the income acquired in Ghana, might never be in the position to build a 'decent house' on their own, if they do not indulge in some kinds of cheating, bribery, and corruption. The 'decent house' here can be a complete house, which has access to a pipe borne water, toilet (water closet), and electricity. Even if the house is incomplete, just only a few rooms, access to the facilities mentioned above might fit into the description of a 'decent house'. Except one is a private business person and/or cocoa farmer in Ghana, who is known to be successful, and for that matter could be expected to be capable of putting up a 'decent house, any other person who puts up a 'decent house' stands to be suspected of having indulged in some corrupt deals. People point to most 'decent houses' and say that it is only those Ghanaians that live or have lived in the Diaspora that own those houses. All this also reinforces the relevance of making the journey to the Diaspora, once in one's life time.

One social change that also needs be mentioned here is the emerged religious dynamism. The rate at which various churches have sprung up in Ghana should lead one to ponder over why all these numerous churches and what do they have in common? Common with all the churches is that they all seem to base their teachings, values and beliefs from the Holy Bible. Different with the churches can be, for example, how they have come into being, who the leaders are, and how they organize and conduct their respective worships. While some traditional churches such as the Roman Catholic Church and the Anglican Church have hierarchical organisations that are there to oversee that priests to lead churches, for instance, would be ordained only after some formal training, some of the newly emerged churches in Ghana have priests or leaders that ordained themselves. The self-ordained priest might have broken away from some traditional church because his or her values and/or beliefs might no longer be congruent with those of the former church. The self-ordained priest may even posit that he or she has got 'a call' to organize and/or lead a church. Once this self-ordained priest succeeds in establishing a church, much vigour is exerted to win and to retain members.

The trend that has been very remarkable with the newly emerged churches is the feeling of 'togetherness' that make them spend hours and hours together at church times, at conventions and the like. Some can even go to church and/or 'all night' gatherings every blessed day and stay on for some lengthy times. This is a marked social change that demands that one needs to be an insider in order to be able to understand why the church members do what they do. A story is told about a soldier (a captain) in Kumasi that went to a church and demanded that the worship be brought to an end because they had been worshiping for a very long time. Perhaps the soldier might have had a wife in the congregation or wanted the people to end the worship and go out to do some communal work (what exactly brought the soldier there can best be told by others; this is just a reconstruction as I heard the story). Incidentally, a serious fight ensued, as the soldier went into the congregation, and in the struggle the soldier was killed. The news of the dramatic and tragic incident reached the Kumasi military barracks. In retaliation for the soldier's death, soldiers were commanded to go and storm the church. The scene that developed afterwards, numerous arrests, molestations, torture and so on, was unforgettable for the many that witnessed that. The priest of the church in question was burnt to death amidst thousands of people in the centre of the Kumasi main lorry station.

In spite of the above isolated, but tragic, incident, the momentum of the growth of new churches goes on unabated. Besides, the spiritual element in their pursuit, the new churches can be also seen as a channel through which the members build social bonds with each other. Many of the new churches have also been internationalized. Some of the leaders of the new churches have realized that many Ghanaians might want to seek after some spiritual meaning of their existence and also establish strong social contacts with fellow Ghanaians and/or some church members in the Diaspora. A visit in Germany in recent time, 2004, reviewed that there are about more than sixty different Ghanaian churches in the country. As most churches are organized on some unique values and beliefs, one's encounter with one's countryman or woman, especially the most religious one, would affect behaviour.

One day I was invited by a fellow Ghanaian family, both of us living in the Diaspora, to some kind of socialisation in the evening where we talked and had dinner together. My host also invited a Ghanaian family at the same time as I was a guest then. We had a very good start, conversing a lot about our mother land, Ghana, making some jokes about the way we look back to Ghana and analyze things, wearing the Diaspora spectacle. The evening seemed to have gone the way we all wanted and/or expected, until it came to the time to serve some drinks. My host knew that I drink alcohol, although I am a Christian, a staunch believer in Christ and a member of the Roman Catholic Church. I accepted the offer with much delight and I hope that my host was also very happy because I liked what they offered me. The other Ghanaian family (a couple), also guests, belonged to the same church as our host. They were members of the Seventh Day Adventist Church. Based on their values and/or beliefs, alcohol is not good for a Christian. Because of their religious values and belief, the other guests went for a non-alcoholic beverage. It came to the turn of our host (the couple and their children) to have some drinks as well so that all of us could propose a toast. Unfortunately, our host did pour to themselves a soft drink, called CIDER with about one and a half or two percent alcohol content. On seeing that our host had poured CIDER with that very little alcohol content to the family members, especially to the children, the man of the family that was there as guests burst out into anger and asked our host this question. "Are you going to drink alcohol and especially the children? The man who put up the question and our host belonged to the same church so the former was expecting that they lived according to their beliefs or whatever. I was a Ghanaian but I could not have a share of mind with these people. Religion made us differ, although all of us are Christians. The atmosphere that we were in naturally became negatively affected.

The Seventh Day Adventist Church is an old denomination, yet here was a member that clinched strictly to their teachings and wanted to correct any improper behaviour. In many of the newly founded churches in Ghana too the members have strict codes of conduct such as abhorrent of alcohol, what hair style, especially women, should wear, the type of dress to put on and so on. It is important to know these trends so that one does not become embarrassed in any encounter with fellow Ghanaians as I did when I met someone who did not think that it was proper for our host to have a drink that contained one and half or two percent alcohol.

Another area which has caught my interest and analysis is how we used to mourn and/or pay our last respect to a family member that has died. This is a social arrangement that has changed markedly over the years. The use of colour is very important for every culture. Colours can signify many things, from aesthetic expression (beauty) to serious connotations such as signifying death and mournful and/or liberation period, for example. I would like to focus briefly on how the use of the colours red and black to signify that our people have lost someone pervaded for many decades. The colours black and red were for a very long time the symbols of mourning someone that had departed for eternity. The sight of someone, especially an adult, dressed in our traditional black or red clothes would fill the observer with the thoughts and/or feelings of death. However, white would produce thoughts and feelings about happiness and joy (e.g. a weeding, a marriage, and a new person has been born). Therefore at burials and funeral celebrations, family members and well-wishers that join the former in mourning the dead person would be expected to be in red or black clothes, be you a child or and adult, a man or woman, a church-goer or non-church-goer. This tradition persisted for a very long time. I have been in the Diaspora since the later part of the seventies. The first time that I realized that the colours, black and red, worn to convey a message about a death and a mourning period was changing was when my own father died and a funeral celebration was held on his behalf, in the early 1990s. During the preparations for the funeral celebration, all grandchildren to my late father were asked to put on white clothes, irrespective of whether they were children or adults. I had travelled from the Diaspora to attend the funeral celebration in question so I questioned why white coloured clothes should be used at my father's funeral. I was told then that that was the trend, a social change that I knew nothing of.

In the 21st century, too, this white colour in combination with the black and red are used to mourn our dead ones. When I tried to seek some meaning and or explanation for the use of the white colour, some tried to tell me that it is all the influence of the churches. The churches that have sprung up in the Ghanaian society are very dynamic and very well organized so their influence are felt in many spheres of the society. I have no problem with that. But it is just that we must be able to map out the changes and the forces underlying those changes. This is important because such knowledge would help us to get to the cause of a social episode, which brings about positive or negative changes in the society. Once that is know, we might be able to go to the root of the problem and try to solve that or build upon positive changes. Besides the Christians, there are Moslems and Traditional worshippers. Islam has, for long, exerted influence on their members in areas such as drinking habits and burial and funeral arrangements. The Moslems are forbidden to drink alcohol and do not also waste time and much resource in burial and funeral arrangements, as the traditional religion and some Christian groups would tolerate. The change that this Islam religion has produced in some Ghanaians is the doing away with the traditional way of mourning and/or organizing funeral celebrations. The use of alcohol, red and black dresses, rituals that are entrenched in most Ghanaian traditions, at burials and funeral celebrations have not been the practice of the Moslems. With the influence of the various religions, it would not be correct to say that Ghanaians have common traditions and/or customs; it will depend upon the situation and the dominating religion behind some social activities.

Since the Christians far outnumber other religious bodies in the Ghanaian society, their influence on the behaviour of their members and on the society, as a whole, is tremendous. In recent times, one would observe that many churches in our big cities have religious sermons during the week days and at weekends; what a practice? Are such church-goers not working in some companies or in some public services? Are they all self-employed and have the means to stay away from work and go to worship instead? Are most of the church-goers (going to church day and night throughout the week) unemployed so that going to church is a way to finding meaning to the hard life and seek some spiritual help to overcome that? Are the churches filling an essential social function, which our politicians (those who have the power to decide in which direction the society should go) have failed to deliver to the people. The church may be seen as the 'giver of spiritual strength and hope to withstand abject poverty, mass unemployment, corruption and cheating and other unacceptable developments. Taken together, the rulers, on whom power and resources have been conferred to bring about justice and equitable distribution, have capitulated to the trend that has split the Ghanaian society into two main classes, "Ebi te yie" versus "Ebi inte yie" (the haves versus the have-nots). These questions, when answered would help us to know whether or not such social changes are positive or negative to the entire society now and in the future, if such changes persist.

Economic Detachment

In almost all societies, social changes may affect and be affected by other changes. The Ghanaian society is undergoing some economic changes that need be analysed too. Ghana is a place where about 70 percent of the population lives in the rural areas. Job opportunities for many people in the rural areas are virtually none. And it is not all that have the financial resources to buy a piece of land and till that for agricultural activities. It is not uncommon that many are in the rural areas doing practically nothing. Some survive because a few members of the extended family might share with them whatever they obtain from their meagre farm proceeds. Others are expecting some favours from family members that live in some larger cities in Ghana but visit their villages. Anyone who returns from the Diaspora, a native of a certain village, will like to pay a visit to his or her birth place (a rural area). The news of the person's presence in a certain village (one's birth place) may draw many people to the visiting native. The change, very sad and embarrassing, is that the people that throng to you to greet you may be old friends, relatives and non-relatives, young and old people who all come not only to greet and to chat but to ask for money or help of some kind. Sadly and unfortunately, the person from the Diaspora has become a symbol for wealth and as such people come to him or her to partake of the wealth. One may try to give money or some presents to as many people as possible that reach up to him or her. But how many can you satisfy, when confronted with many hands? I invited my German-born friend of mine to visit Ghana with me in the year 2003. He witnessed how a lot of people came to me, both in the biggest cities and in the rural areas that we visited. I have relatives, friends and acquaintances in most of the areas we visited. My friend saw the seen and jokingly called me "social welfare office". Yes, I deserved that description because all who came to me expected to get money from me; and they were very many.

The above scene also reinforces the perception that travelling to the Diaspora is worth all the investments one would make in order to be able to make that journey. Believe it or not, you would try to let the people know that you do not have money to share with all.

They would not want to believe that. Many would bring very serious problems before you, sickness, lack of food, etc., and would not leave you until you do something about their problems. It is a very embarrassing scene. And as said earlier on, many are living under abject poverty so the dependence ratio (many living on a few) is extremely high. I have been visiting Ghana almost every second year, if nothing prevents me from doing that, but the situation described is getting worst and worst. Most people are living far below the poverty line so many have been made to beg for their survival. The solution to get out of this abject poverty, as many see it, is to migrate to the urban areas and/or to the Diaspora in search of better living conditions.

Unfortunately, job opportunities in the urban areas are very limited. Many that come there get frustrated and might take to all sorts of activities, including perhaps crimes. In recent times rampant and brutal armed robbery in the urban cities has become a common place, something that was unknown in the past. If there were some armed robberies at all in the past, they were not on the same magnitude and sophisticatedly organised as in recent times. Our cities are over-crowded with many people doing nothing but just waiting for some job opportunities to come their way. Many young children have no interest and motivation in going to school. Their parents cannot afford the cost involved in educating a child nowadays. Many children have taken to the streets of our urban areas, selling whatever they lay their hands on. Sadly enough, you would find school going-children on the streets of our big cities selling some handful of chewing gums, handkerchiefs, sweets, and so on. Most of the people who are discontent with the type of the life they are leading in Ghana are constantly seeking way to travel to the Diaspora. An unfortunate development, thinking about the plight of the many that live under abject poverty, is how some people exploit the situation of the poor ones. Some call themselves 'contractors' who offer to help people obtain passport and/or visas against very high fees. Why should any person lead a fellow Ghanaian to obtain a common passport against a fee, besides the legal fees that one would be made to pay at the ministry of foreign affairs or its equivalent? Is not passport a basic need for every Ghanaian? Should the society encourage this shameful exploitation of the needy? Yes, this has been going on for many years. During the time I was preparing to travel to the Diaspora in the 1970s this anti-social practice, helping someone to get a passport for a fee, was well entrenched in the society. Almost three decades after that the same practice is in existence. Why has not this practice changed then over the years, in spite of all the positive changes that governments preach? This is because some notorious and scrupulous people are making money out of that.

People also go to the extent of collecting huge amount of money from some innocent, but the struggling poor, people and promise to help them obtain visas to the Diaspora. Many people have lost their hard-won money as the result of such malpractices from fellow Ghanaians. A recent example, in the year 2005, is where about 10 or twenty queen mothers from various areas in Ghana were promised visas by a woman contractor to enable them to pay a visit to Queen Elisabeth in England. These Ghanaian queen mothers, who saw that chance as a great privilege to visit Queen Elisabeth for consultation and/or sharing of ideas, together paid thousands of dollars to the self-imposed contractor. The contractor used the money but was unable to obtain visas for the victims. These victims, queen mothers, lodged a complaint to the court. How many common people can take their criminal visa contractors to court? Where is the Ghanaian society heading? Certain organized crimes, such as visa-contracting, passport-contracting, have been going on for ages. And now some are using violence to get what they need, the increased armed robbery. There is nothing more 'infectious' than relative poverty. Relative poverty has to do with comparing one's situation with someone else's. This is because one feels that he or she is on the same scale as the comparable person. For example, they belong to the same social class, have had the same education and have even been struggling in the past together. But, of no apparent reasons, the fellow one has been comparing himself or herself to starts doing wonderful things, although he or she has no visible job. This comparison might drive many people, those who cannot live decent lives because their 'comparables' are doing better, to take to criminal acts in order to become rich quickly too. That is why you see so many false passport contractors, visa-contractors, clearing agencies (at our harbours) and contractors who help someone to get his or her indenture and lease papers on a bought piece of land processed. How long do we have to live with these 'empty' and unproductive activities in the society? Positive changes going on in Ghana have not touched these areas that set our development back. Many are making money without doing any productive things. They send bad and/or wrong signals to others. It does not pay to do hard work in Ghana these days. Think about lotto and their various 'lotto-doctors' that sell numbers. What is this nonsense? If such fake lotto-doctors know which numbers will win, why would they sell them?

It is not uncommon that lack of employment for the masses, inability to meet the most basic needs in the society such as proper health care, cost of education of children, decent roof over the head and proper feeding of yourself and dependents are all driving some able-bodied people to risk all they possess to sell to raise money for the hope of leaving the country, to Europe, North America, Asia and Libya. This rational behaviour of many people, running away from hopelessness and abject poverty, is not something typical of Ghanaians. The world has over the years seen mass exodus of people from one area into another, the reasons of which have some similarities as the contemporary migration from areas of deprivation and/or disasters (most of which are man-made). Look around you and you would find white people in Australia, New Zealand, Tasmania, USA, Canada, Latin America, and South Africa. At some point in time, in 1800, the trend of the time was the mass migration of the white people into such areas. To some extent, this trend continues even until today, under a quite different condition. Thus, one could be encouraged to migrate to Canada, USA, South Africa and Australia, for example, if it is proved beyond doubt that the immigrant can contribute towards the host country's development. Come with a huge amount of capital and 'top-of the world expertise' in some defined areas of importance, and the host country would welcome you. Look around you and you would also find some Asians, Africans and Arabs, for example, scattered all over the world too. In mankind's struggle to migrate from areas of hardships (poverty, persecution and misery) to areas of hope and affluence, a development has been set in where boundaries have been erected very tightly around almost all habitable areas. The boundaries have the ultimate role to limit further mobility of mankind from places of deprivation, for example, to places pregnant with all essentials of life.

The change where the gates to affluent areas have been closed to unfortunate people wanting to emigrate from misery has not been seen by leaders of some under-developed countries. Or they have seen the change but they just ignore it because they think there is nothing they can do about the change. Instead, people are left to their own fate to take whatever risk there is to be able to go through the boundaries elected by the rich countries. For over almost two hundred years ago, most European emigrants to North America, for example, for better life were helped by very well-organized institutions to be able to do the journey. In almost all museums in most cities in Europe one can read reports on the organized migration into the new world of hope and richness. The poor areas of today are unfortunately having no such organizations to help potential emigrants to travel to their dream countries. What obtains is the emergent of corrupt markets where some fellow country people dupe their own country people by charging exorbitant fees for 'faked visas' that might help the victims, hopefully get to some 'promised' land. Some are smuggled under very inhuman conditions across countries. Many die as the result, never making the dream journey they set themselves to do; what a tragedy! Some young people from Ghana, who set off on foot from Libya with the aim of crossing to Europe were so worn out by hunger and what not that they, died on the way. Reports were also made of about twenty Chinese people that were smuggled in a container to England. On arrival, almost all of them were discovered dead. Yet these tragic incidents do not deter many to try the 'dubious' way of making the journey to the Diaspora. Isn't it sad to hear that one emigrant, caught at the boarder of Spain and threatened to be sent back to where he came from preferred to die instantly than to be sent back home?

Why would a person prefer to die, instead of being returned to his or her country of birth? Yes, it has most to do with our attitude towards failure. On his/her return, virtually no one would sympathize with him/her, slapping him or her on the shoulders to say that it was a trial, 'that is not the end of the world'. Instead, he or she would be a subject of ridicule by many people. The government has no plan for people that ventured to leave Ghana to seek better opportunities elsewhere but fail to achieve that goal. Once deported to Ghana, for example, there is the likelihood that the 'deportee' might even be thrown to jail instead of the government doing something to re-habilitate and/or to re-integrate such a person that has gone through such traumas or ordeals. Many have risked making the journey to the Diaspora on their own. For most Ghanaians in the Diaspora, the contacts between the motherland never sever. They know the plight of the people (people living in a society plagued with poverty and mass unemployment, for example) they left behind. Some will remit relatives constantly. This is something acknowledged and appreci-ated by the government. According to the government (recent gov-ernment of President Kuffour in the 21st century), one third of Ghana's foreign exchange earnings come from transfers from Gha-naians living in the Diaspora. This is/was the first time a president of Ghana, has officially appreciated and commended Ghanaians in the Diaspora for their contribution to Ghana's development. Transfers from Ghanaians in the Diaspora to Ghana have been going on long before President's Kuffour's government came to power. All this also would have to let us look into the political changes that Ghana has been going through over the years.

Political Detachment

There is no area that I feel much more detached from my country of birth than the political arena. The then Gold Coast, which is called Ghana since the country's independence from the colonial power, the British government, underwent an enormous transforma-tion. Under the British government rule, although our chieftaincy system had a role to play, the imposition of British political system (with its values, norms, and traditions) on Gold Coast relegated the country into a structure that was neither known nor practised in then Gold Coast nor in Great Britain. Long before the British people suc-ceeded to colonize Gold Coast, there was no unified country called Gold Coast. What obtained were a number of small 'Kingdoms', each of which had its own governance structure (s). For example, the Ashanti Kingdom was organized around chieftaincy systems, with an overall King that reigned over the various Ashanti chief-doms. Thus, chiefs in various areas in Ashanti were enstooled according to some well-organized norms and practices. A chief once enstooled, would have to be brought to the overall Ashanti King for approval and/or 'ordainment', a practice without which no one could be a chief anywhere in the Ashanti Kingdom.

Still dwelling on the Ashanti Kingdom, the King of Ashanti as well as the sub-chiefs in the Ashanti Kingdom were looked upon and regarded as people whose ancestors have excelled in contributing to the existence and/or well-being of the people under their respective jurisdiction. At the time when many Kingdoms were going to war with each other, for treasures and whatever, the Ashanti King for example had to lead his people for war and against war. These activities could lead to the expansion and/or the defeat of a Kingdom. And all wars were fought for power and influence over other Kingdoms and their people. The defeated would have to pay taxes and/or perform certain activities for example. It was therefore very important to see that whoever is enstooled as a King or a chief would have to have the qualities to lead his people to prosperity, against invasion and internal security and harmony. That was one of the reasons why the ancestors of the present Ashanti King had to lead and/or mobilize the people of Ashanti to fight the British colonialists' invasion of the Ashanti territory, until the former was defeated in the 1900.

The Ashanti King or the sub-chiefs of Ashanti are bequeathed with power to see to the welfare of the people he rules over. It was not uncommon that the chiefs, the first to settle in a particular place, develop and defend it, would help every one that migrated into the chief's territory. The help could be in the form of giving the 'immigrant' a piece of land to farm on and even a temporary place to live. My grandmother, for example, migrated from her place of birth, Adeesena, into a place called Nyinahin. My grandmother, of blessed memory, told me about the assistance she received from the then chief of the Nyinahin town, especially in acquiring a farming land and protecting her against litigious people who, after a while tried to take away my grandmother's farm land from her. The chief and his elders (those assisting him) could settle disputes, could punish and also reward people, all in commensurate to what the situation is/was. It was the chief's duty also to organize communal labour and so on to help develop the society. So it has always been a very important institution, the chieftaincy that has been preserved over the years. A number of people, those that have also excelled in some society contributions, although might not be royal family members as the King or the chief and his relatives, could and are appointed to assist the chief to rule the people. All this knowledge was something the British colonialists could not ignore about the role of our chief in the society. When they succeeded to colonize the whole of Gold Coast under one governance structure, the British rule system, they used our chiefs to assist in ruling the people. The British authorities knew that the Kings of the various parts of Gold Coast (the Ashanti King and/or Kingdom is just given here as example; there were other Kings and Kingdoms in the Gold Coast) waged authority over their people; the people owed absolute allegiance to their various Kings and/or chiefs. The British government therefore maintained this traditional line of authority and ruled through them, a system that was coined as the 'indirect rule'. I would leave these historical issues to historians and/or political scientists because they might be in the better position to give an account of the evolution of the political developments in Ghana.

Although the British used the 'indirect rule system, to govern Gold Coast, a system that accorded our local rulers some influence in helping to shape the destinies of their people, what the people of Gold Coast were subjected to was contrary to what British people were exposed to. For example, British people could elect their own political rulers, while the people of Gold Coast had governors and district commissioners all appointed from England to come down to rule over the people they knew nothing of. While almost all revenues obtained in England were used to develop the place, the substantial part of the revenues from the Gold Coast was sent to develop England. It came to a point that the people of the Gold Coast could not allow the colonial masters to siphon the revenues from Gold Coast, for example, to England, while the people lived in abject poverty. Hence, in the later part of the 1930s and in the 1940s, some inhabitants of the then Gold Coast (do not want to name any one here for the fear that I might miss some of them) stood up and demanded independence from the British government. Again, the historians would know better than me. My point here is that the people of Gold Coast had to realize that foreign domination could no longer be tolerated.

At long last Ghana, the then Gold Coast under the British, attained independence in 1957. What all hoped for was that the political rulers that emerged could lead and/or direct the country towards, peace, actual freedom and prosperity. The modern rulers in Ghana did not involve the chiefs so much, as the British people did by the use of the 'indirect rule', in their administrative arrangements. Although the chiefs and/or the Kings still exist, their influence on the people had been summarily reduced. Government administrators had to assume virtually all the mandatory powers to direct and guide what and how development projects in the society, for example, had to be carried on. There were times that even chieftaincy matters had to be the dictate of the ruling government. It was possible, for instance, for a royal chief to be removed and a non-royal person, because of political manoeuvres, could be put on a throne by a government. This was something that not only disrespected the people, but also almost destroyed the very social governance which the people have much hope in and are loyal to. This politicization of the chieftaincy system in Ghana, at some point in our history, undermined the social structure that the people had known and treasured over years.

The role that a chief of a people had been playing, as discussed elsewhere in this book, was not appreciated and incorporated into the modern Ghanaian politics, as the British did during the colonial period. Some governments, especially those that believed in state socialism could not see that the chiefs, when properly integrated into the modern Ghanaian socio-economic and political development could be of great help. The high allegiance and/or loyalty and trust, which some chiefs enjoyed from their people was a threat to some governments. Hence, the role and/or the positions of chiefs were undermined. Political parties that were in existence, before and a few years after independence were also suppressed. Already in the early 1960s, the ruling government could not share power or responsibility in the development of Ghana with any party, organization and/or individual that did not have a 'share of mind' with the ruling government regarding the direction Ghana should go. This totalitarianism bred not only enmity, but brought about active squabbles that sought to destroy political opponents. This development led to some people being thrown to detection, without trial, and others had to flee the country for their lives.

Unfortunately, the Ghana political scene had become a battle ground to brutally fight for political influence. From the period of independence, 1957 until today, the following governments have come to power, some through very brutal and illegal ways: 1957-1966 civilian government, 1966-1969 military government, 1969-1972 civilian government, 1972-1978 military government, 1978-1979 military government, June 1979-September 1979 military government, 1979-1981 civilian government, 1981-1993 military government, 1993-2000 civilian government, 2000-2004 civilian, and 2004- civilian. These developments have had their negative impacts. Ghana has witnessed so much of her valuable resources, human and material, being wasted into fighting internally for power instead of a constructive development of the country, where all and sundry could leverage their capabilities to complement each other in that effort. The resources have not been invested in developmental ventures that would have lifted the country from where the colonialists left us. The same colonialists ruled India, Pakistan, Singapore, Malaysia, Hong Kong, and Taiwan, for example. All these countries have in some way, been able to prove to the colonialists that they are capable to rule over their own country, raising the living standard of their people better than it was under the colonial rule. The same cannot be said of Ghana.

We spend too much time undermining, fighting and sabotaging one another. Compromising with someone whose ideas, values, interests and wishes differ from oneself seems to be a hard thing for our leaders to do. This trait of self-indulgence and 'Mister Know all' attitude of our leaders have done more harm than good for the development of the country. In Ghana, people have heard some leaders claiming that they held Ghana in their hands like some one holding an egg in the hand. Just as the egg being held in the hand can be squeezed to break, he could also do whatever he liked with Ghana. Some would also ask: "To whom do we have to hand over power", when pressures mounted on them to release power to others? Someone, along the way, attempted to create a one party state, all from his own personal values, beliefs and conviction of what he thought was good for Ghana. And we have also had leaders who did not get pressed to bring to thorough investigations, why and how three Supreme Court judges were captured from their respective homes and brought to somewhere in the open air to be murdered.

If judges could be rounded up and killed, how much more does one expect of an ordinary man's protection and security by the state's security net? Yes, we have modern Ghanaian leaders that do not do much to protect the lives of the citizens. After the mysterious murder of the three judges, the killings have not ceased. A number of women were also discovered murdered in the street of our capital town, Accra, in the 21st century. When such heinous crimes came into the notice of the public, an ex-president came out to say that he knew the people behind the killings of the women but he was not going to release those names, until a lie-detective machine was used on him and those he suspected. Or unless the authorities brought him, the ex-president, and the suspects to a local shrine (at Antoa in the Ashanti region), he would not name any one. What do the ex-president and the present Government think about Ghanaians? Isn't it the moral obligation of the ex-president and the current Government to uncover the atrocities meted out to innocent Ghanaians? The safety net in Ghana is in danger. Not only are many people without jobs and are living in poverty, protection of life is not there. Whatever the causes of these killings, Ghanaians have the right to know that. But who is there to help the people with such vital information? It looks as if our political machinery has broken down.

What Ghana needs are leaders that have the flair that excites and stimulates the people, in all sectors of the society, to help develop the country; fighting poverty, combat crimes against fellow Ghanaians and creating a better Ghana for posterity to come would need someone that can move the people towards that goal. As at now, at the time of writing this book, 2005, it looks as if Ghana has no consolidating sense of purpose or direction. Go to the Internet, GhanaWeb.com for example; get hold of some local news papers and all one reads are reports about poverty, increasing armed robbery, Ghanaians fleeing hardships stranded in the Sahara desert, people of high positions embezzling tax payers' money, and ex-president and the sitting president raining insults on each other. At one time (in the 1960s) in the history of the country, active promotion and/or creation of infant industries, an example of a consolidating sense of purpose and direction, made it possible for some noteworthy Ghanaian-owned firms to start, grow and flourish; such firms served as import-substitution producers. They helped save foreign currencies, which might have gone into imports; this also strengthened the value of the local currency.

Another example of a consolidating sense of purpose and direction was illustrated by the mobilization of the people to produce goods and services for themselves (a national move that was labelled "operation feed yourself"). All this was possible because there was a genuine commitment from the leaders at those times. They encouraged and supported the people in the collective strive to work towards self-sufficiency. But unfortunately, such exemplary attempts towards self-sufficiency had no effective programmes or systems in place to ensure sustainability over the years. Many such efforts collapsed as their initiators were forced out of office and those who took over power did not see the need to continue. The sad thing is that new leaders who mounted the platform of power, but refused or failed to continue with developments that seemed to have worked and involved the people, could not come with alternative solutions. Ghana's developmental efforts began to falter.

Having leaders that have the flair to mobilize all and sundry to leverage their capabilities in solving societal problems has been the yardstick on which leaders come to power and/or are evaluated in almost all countries that have created better and enviable living standards for their people. Hence, it is not uncommon to see some ruling parties of a country, sometimes in co-operation with coalition partners in parliament, allocate resources to accomplish, for instance, some of the following:

As I Journey Along

- Improve upon health care system for all
- Improve upon living conditions for the handicapped people
- Improve upon education and making it possible for all children to get education
- Care for the unemployed
- Support and fund research and development projects that will uplift all sectors of the society
- Provide resources for the law enforcing agencies to maintain law and order

And above all, provide jobs and/or encourage industrial activities that can offer jobs.

Isn't it ironic and quite disappointing to see that, in Ghana in the 21st century, the ex-president and the sitting president invest too much time and energy in personally attacking each other, day in and day out? This behaviour of people of such higher level of the political ladder in the society has prompted chiefs, clergymen and/or church leaders and ordinary people to also spend time to appeal to the presidents to bury their differences. What behoves of the presidents, as most of them advise, is to provide examples worthy of emulation and also to engage in mobilising the people towards seeking solutions to the numerous problems facing Ghana. If higher ranking individuals, ex-president and the sitting president, have problems in respecting each other and each other's values and beliefs, in compromising on a number of issues that would make Ghana move forward, go to the extent of insulting each other, for no apparent reason, and do not reflect on what impact their behaviour might have on the ordinary citizen, then, the political landscape in Ghana is under the care of leaders who are very indifferent to the woes of the country. Sometimes one is inclined to believe that the political culture that has not been well-developed, looking at political evolution in the country, could be the plausible explanation for the political chaos that prevails in Ghana. As discussed somewhere in this book, the country has undergone colonization. It has been ruled by military people who came to power through violence; recall that the military has ruled Ghana, on a number of periods, more than civilians have done. Some civilian individuals, who weird absolute power and could not think of separation of powers as something for

Ghana and her people, have also left their influence on the political culture bestowed on 'modern' Ghana. Ghana is yet to have leaders who lead a team of people, which will all help bring Ghana to the path of sustainable development. The masses would follow leaders who prove to be selfless, inspiring and committed to direct the people into prosperity. With this background, I dive into trying to understand why things are as they are now in Ghana, discussing things from the Diaspora spectacles that I have on.

Understanding Things As They Are In Ghana

Perception on Ghana-Made Good/Services

I cannot help but to take my point of departure from the colonial heritage that has been bestowed on Ghanaians. The colonial administrators introduced the payment of taxes and levies towards the development of the country. Unfortunately, much of the state revenues, obtained from the economic activities such as mining, timber production and cocoa farming (the three main revenue earners), were sent to develop England instead. Instead of developing some basic industrial infrastructure, which could enhance local production and sales of most goods and services, Ghana was left to thrive on the under-developed agricultural economy. Many basic goods and services that Ghanaians have over the years enjoyed mostly come from overseas. Sectors such as transportation, health, education, entertainment (musical devices, movies, etc), communication, manufacturing and retailing have all, since the colonial period and the present time, been heavily reliant on foreign inputs. The dependence on foreign inputs is so overwhelming that efforts by some Ghanaians to produce and market goods and services are matched against the foreign comparable offers. A Ghanaian that is trying to produce shoes certainly will also have to depend on some foreign production inputs, for example, glues, leather, nails and even packaging materials. The Ghanaian that usually starts investment with some meagre resources cannot obtain adequate quality materials, which will enable him/her produce large quantities (scale economies will bring cost per unit down), at a lower cost and at some acceptable quality that the potential customer will want to pay money for. After all, having been used to foreign taste, due to the colonial heritage, and once the well-packaged and cheap foreign goods and services are over-flooded in the marketplace, the Ghanaian offer has no market chance. The belief that all that is foreign is better than any Ghanaian product, whether that is true or not is debatable, is the number one enemy or a major competitive weapon that any Ghanaian business person that starts production from the scratch would have to fight to overcome.

Creating domestic industrial capacity that would help produce 'input-output' goods or services for Ghana's self-sufficiency was realized by the Ghana Government that inherited power from the colonial masters. However, the development of the industrial capacity leaned towards the dictates of state socialism. Instead of developing, in parallel, state enterprises and also encouraging and supporting local private entrepreneurial efforts, the latter was virtually discriminated. The wisdom of the time was to promote collective ownership, production and distribution of goods and services. Private ventures, though existed, they were marginalized. Some scarce and critical preferential financial resources were directed to State Enterprises. As reported elsewhere (Fieldhouse, 1978, p.412), the economic climate in Ghana deteriorated already in the 1960s because the country suffered from an accelerated adverse balance of trade. Yes, Ghana has for long been relying on foreign goods and services. Successive governments would intervene, especially when the country's balance of trade (the country's trade with other countries must be balanced) is negative, by introducing some trade restrictions such as high import duties, imposing quotas for certain imports, and even banning certain imports and encouraging and supporting domestic production. Ghana has tried this last measure once in the 1960s, with some mixed results.

At a certain point in time, Ghana had some food processing industries such as Ghana Industrial Holding Corporation (GIHOC), Tema Food Processing Corporation and other industries (e.g. Textile factories). These were domestic firms that were brought about as the result of direct government involvement and massive resources, import-substituting projects. The efforts of private firms have been marginalized, as said before. How far a country can use such instruments such as import-substitution policy to restrict imports and impose controls is summarily reduced in the modern globalization drive, where liberalization is the rule rather than exception. Where Ghana is not able to use some restrictions to protect domestic production from foreign competition and, for that matter, limit people's consumption of foreign goods and services, which make the people dependent on foreign offers, Ghanaians that would want to compete with the foreign goods and services have a real problem. The belief and the attitude among many people are that Ghanaian goods and services are inferior.

The people that have such negative perceptions of Ghanaian-made goods and services cannot be blamed for what they believe in. The people suffer already from low wages, so whenever they are buying some essential goods and services, they opt for something for the money, not any shoddy offer. So even if, I or many others, wearing the Diaspora glasses, would suggest that Ghanaians have to be patriotic, we have got to think about the situational variables that underlie such preferences. If we want Ghanaians to buy Ghanaian goods, we would have to embark on nation-wide research and development to help upgrade the technologies of our domestic firms. They do not have to produce "new to the world product or services", not many firms in developed world do that either. However, whatever they set themselves to produce, they have to put the customer in the centre and ask simple questions such as these: are we offering benefits and/or value to satisfy the needs and wants of the customer? Where and how will these benefits and values be delivered? Will the customer be able to pay for the benefits? There can be several other important questions, which need be answered to help the seller determine whether or not his or her offers will be preferred by some customers.

For many domestic firms, the lack of some production inputs

such as machinery, industrial lubricants and even raw materials would have to be imported. The hard currencies to be used to import production inputs are not easy to come by, so firms may improvise and use anything at hand to produce something; the results of which is poor quality and poor presentation. If domestic firms do not get some help, in the form of research and development activities, competitive bank credit and access to most basic production inputs internally, Ghanaian firms, with their offers, would not be able to wash away the negative image (the perception that Ghanaian goods are inferior) that seems to cause Ghanaian customers to turn their back to Ghana-made goods and services. Are there some explanations for the poor performance of the Ghanaian manufacturer relative to his or foreign competitors? Faced with competitive pressures from imported goods, particularly, many Ghanaian-owned firms, even the state-owned ones that enjoyed massive preferential financial support, for example, from the government, closed down in the 1980s. As reported elsewhere (Tangari, 1992), some import-substitution manufacturing firms (garments, leather-processing, cosmetics and plastics, and food processing firms) have closed down, as the trade in Ghana was liberalised since the early 1980s until recent time.

The last textile factory in Jaupong is yet to close down, if the government does not intervene to save the close down and loss of 100s of jobs. If the state monopolies such as the production and supply of electricity and water were to be liberalised, as the same fate that faced those state-owned corporations that are wiped out of the market because of increased competition, they would not be able to match rivalry. Ask any Ghanaian customer about how satisfied he or she is with the purchase and consumption of electricity and water, and the answer would be very shocking. Incessant irregular supply of electricity and water, but with no apology, explanation, and compensation, can only be a practice by corporations that have state monopolies. The worst of it all is that, whether regular supply or not, consumers believe that they are paying the same amount of bills regularly. How could the state back such inhuman treatment by sellers? If the state were forced by some exogenous factors, as it has happened to some state enterprises, to deregulate the electricity and the water markets respectively, would such corporations that do not know anything about customer-orientation have any customer in the face of competition? The answer is clear; no.

Mismanagement:
Why Things Are As They Are

State-owned enterprises that have once been perceived to be the driving forces that will enable Ghana achieve self-sufficiency and, for that matter, offer job opportunities and a better living standard for all became the arena on which political leaders could display their prowess. The management team of such important state-owned enterprises had little to do with people that had the competence, dedication and the innovative drive to run those enterprises. Rather, political affiliation (in the case of politicians ruling Ghana) and pro-fession and friendship that reflected the organization that ruled the country at the time (here military personnel dominated managerial positions in our enterprises). In the 21st century, the cry on each lip in Ghana is the total mismanagement of our state-owned enterprises. The people now demand the sale of almost all state-owned enter-prises. In the area of the mines, one of the back-bones of the Ghana-ian economy, the development was/is quite disappointing. While in the 1930s Ghana had about 30 gold mines, for example, by 1983, the total number of gold mines in Ghana was only four (see Ghana ex-porters' directory, 1991).

Ghana started with about 20 Black Star ship vessels at the time of independence. Already in the 1980s the ship vessels had decreased to about only four. A recent pain of mismanagement is the Ghana Airways' episode that surfaced in the 21st century. The aircraft was ceased to fly to areas such as German, Hamburg, and the USA, New York, all because the airline had serious safety deficits; some major maintenance work on the airline had long been over due and those ports in question would not risk the lives of people so they forbade the airline to fly to or to land in the respective areas. The Ghana Airways was a very busy airline, which flew almost everyday, mostly with full passengers and/or cargos. Why then did the airline lack resources to undertake safety maintenance? Some people, who through their political connections, controlled the critical resources of the Ghana Airways did not put customer need satisfaction and/or safety first, they used the resources for themselves. Rumours had it that one Minister of Transport could instruct the then Ghana Airways' Office in Baltimore, USA, to pay, on some occasions, 1000s of dollars, from the company's coffers, to the Minister's girl friend. This scandalous incident surfaced in the Ghanaian media and in the Internet, yet little has been done to investigate the matter to ascertain whether or not such an allegation was true. The Ghana Airways, once the proud investment venture in Ghana, became bankrupt in 2004.

All this goes to tell the reader that the type of industrial capacity Ghana has, over the years, been trying to build, lacks what it takes to do the job. It takes, among other things, competitive business climate where private entrepreneurs and state-owned firms compete, side by side or head on, on a fair playground. For example, access to critical resources (e.g. bank credits, foreign exchange for importing critical production inputs, public customers such as government agencies and licences and/or permissions without which many private firms cannot operate efficiently) must not be discriminatory. The firm, be it state-owned or private, must be encouraged and helped to source critical resources at competitive conditions. And there should be clearly formulated government policies to govern industrial activities. With the state-owned enterprises, competence, skills, dedication and problem-solving, and the right attitude rather than tribe, gender, political background, for example, should be the cues for appointing people to lead such enterprises. In some parts of the world, where, state-owned enterprises are properly managed, in developed and in less developed world, they still perform very well, when their state monopolistic positions were deregulated. In Ghana, the state monopolies, when faced with liberalisation, are not able to match market challenges and they close down. If Ghana can have meaningful state-owned corporations to compete alongside with private firms (foreign and indigenous), this is not impossible, let corporations start to learn how to provide value and satisfaction to the customer. For the customer is in the marketplace not to buy the product, electricity or water, but to satisfy a need. What use is it, if there is electricity in a house but there are no lights? There are water closets, water taps and so on, but when the consumer needs water, nothing runs through the pipes or the water closet. These are the issues that Ghanaian firms, private or state-owned, need to address.

One would expect that since Ghana still is an agricultural economy, some progress is being made there. Unfortunately, the answer is no. Since the time of Ghana's independence the export of cocoa, the major foreign earner of the country, has been reserved to the government. There is nothing wrong with that activity of the government, which is supposed to help channel the revenues from cocoa towards the overall development in Ghana. However, one would expect that Ghana would do all it could to maintain and/or defend its position, as far as cocoa production and the revenues thereof are concerned. This would have demanded that Ghana takes good care of its cocoa farmers, their needs and/or their problems, very well so that Ghana's production would always be able to match and/or pre-empt competition from other areas, notably Cote d'Voire, Nigeria and Brazil. Already in the 1970s, Ghanaian farmers faced problems (Roe, 1991) such as lack of financial incentives, unreliable payment procedures, lower producer prices, ageing and diseased trees, shortages of fertilizers and vital pesticides, and poor transport and distribution services.

Again, state monopoly (it is only the government that buys cocoa and exports that) and the fool government representatives make of that monopoly became clear when the military government under John Jerry Rawlings had to send soldiers to go and 'drill' and an ordinary Ghanaian, old, young, weak and strong, to go to villages or cocoa stations to carry cocoa to where they could be on onward transfer to the ports for export. Was it madness to have waited all that long for such an action? People were working under Ghana Cocoa Marketing Board (CMB) or COCOBOD and some other agencies, getting pay to see to the purchase and transportation of cocoa to the ports for export. In any remote village, for example a place with about only ten people, the best house one would find there would be that of the cocoa secretary. The cocoa secretaries, all over in the cocoa producing areas in Ghana, receive regular monthly income. All the various CMB or COCOBOD officers, spread throughout the country, get also regular monthly salaries and some are even having luxurious private cars.

The only time the cocoa farmer receives income is during the time of harvest of cocoa, at most two periods in a year. At the time when the white-colour workers involved in the cocoa business (the various cocoa secretaries and those in the CMB offices) were not having transports to bring the cocoa they had purchased to the ports how were they paid then? And when it became clear that the Rawlings' government could transport the cocoa to the port why did they have to force the ordinary person and not the white-colour workers that directly earned their living from the cocoa business to go and do the carrying of the cocoa? Yes, we sometimes believe in 'command economy', as was practiced under Rawlings for some time, without diving into the real problems facing Ghana. The position of cocoa farmers in Ghana is so devastating that the result has been the ultimate decline in cocoa output in Ghana. In recent times it is reported (Asante et al, 2000) that the mines have taken over cocoa in the earning of foreign currencies for the country. Ghana is no longer the world's leading producer of cocoa, a position the country enjoyed for many years. Some effects of such a development is mass migration of young people from rural areas into urban centres, creating shortages of labour in the cocoa farms and other agricultural activities. If decline in cocoa output goes on 'unhealed', the consequences can be high to bear. The industry gives the most employment to people, a very labour intensive industry.

Our leaders should address this situation; else the consequences of the decline of cocoa output can be serious to bear in the longer perspective. At a certain point in time, when cocoa farming paid off, men and women that were doing cocoa farming worked to grow the business. It was not uncommon to find that a farmer having one or two big farms already in the Ashanti region would move on to the Western region or into Brong-Ahafo region to cultivate additional farms. That was the period when cocoa farmers could live on their income, some building mighty and decent houses (e.g. most mighty houses in the Kumasi Aduma area), and diversifying into other farming activities. Today cocoa farmers are among the underprivi-leged ones in Ghana. Some of the problems facing them have been enumerated above. It is not surprising therefore that recruiting younger generations into cocoa farming, especially those with rural background and have the skills and knowledge in cultivating cocoa, is extremely difficult. Can the civil service organization also have some impact on the struggle to be self-sufficient and enhance the improvement of the living standards of the masses? How does one see Ghanaian civil service organization's behaviour towards the people?

The Ghanaian civil service organization, like any civil service anywhere in the world, is expected to assist whichever government is leading the country to cater to the needs of the people. What makes the civil service special and most essential is that it is a per-manent organization that is in place to serve the people, while gov-ernments will come and go. This civil service anonymity should make any person that happens to work there feel committed, blessed and far more proud; it is a place of office that is not only revered, but offers job security. In a country plagued by mass unemployment, a job secured in the civil service should be so treasured that com-mitment to duty and honestly serving the people should not be tem-pered with. It is the tax payer who is paying for the salaries and, for that matter, giving the civil servants a standard of living. If a civil servant is not accused of a gross misconduct, a misdemeanour that might warrant that his or her continued stay in the service would endanger the service beyond 'repairs', a civil servant cannot be dis-missed; that is what the civil service anonymity implies. The same cannot be said of governments and the politicians working for them (the governments). This should make the civil service a privileged body of organization in a country like Ghana where the majority of the people have never and would never be on any regular pay roll like the people employed in the civil service. What then has made the civil service lose touch with the people?

The Ghanaian civil service has lost touch with the people they are supposed to serve. The various ministries in the country are staffed with people who have pledged to help meet the needs of the masses, a promise, when fulfilled, should guarantee the civil servants their living. Whether it is a colonial heritage or not, the civil service in Ghana, ever since the country's independence, has been accused of massive corruption and bribery. Anybody that has had some encounters with some civil service because of the need of some approvals needed for some activities, licences for some activities, public contracts for some activities, permission for some activities, the list can be long, would testify to how callous and/or indifferent some civil servants could be towards their duty to help solve the person's problem. Why would not some civil servants help solve the people's problem, when the former are approached? Yes, they would not see it as a duty to help solve a problem. For many, it is a chance to earn 'double income'. Mind you, if one goes to a ministry for some help or not, the people working in the ministry would get their monthly income. The same cannot be said of our poor farmers, petty traders and many self-employed people in the society. For them serving whoever comes to them with a problem is a potential asset; for they earn their living from providing value and satisfaction for the people who bring their problems to them. If the farmer does not go to the farm to work and harvest, no money would come from anywhere, unlike the civil servants who would get income if people go to them with their problems or not. To come by easy money, in the form of taking bribes and/or through corruptive activities has gone on for a long time that governments upon governments have given up the fight to rid Ghana clean of this anti-social practices, which has contributed immensely to the country's backwardness.

Governments, as said before, come and go. Yet it is the governments that mount the 'platform of power' to promise the electorate that they would solve the country's problems such as bribery and corruptions. Hence, all they need is the people's mandate to enable them, the governments, take control of the critical resources of the country, which would help them develop the country. The governments also have the power to use sanctions, positive and negative, to reward sectors and the people working in them for creating value sharable among the people. All necessary support, human and materials, be channelled to such areas. Similarly, the government is in the position to punish sectors and the people working in them for engaging in unproductive and/or anti-developmental activities. This can be done by, for example, not channelling public infrastructures financed with scarce public resources to those areas. A government can do all these, if there are clear policies that govern the actions of people, businesses, civil servants and politicians. This will also demand policy implementers, the civil servants, to know their roles and the limit of their influence, if any at all, on the execution of government policies. If government policies, pave the way for some customs officers, some civil servants at the ministry of foreign affairs (especially those working with passports), and some that approve government contracts, for example, to interpret policies (because they are very ambiguous and/or oblique to the ordinary citizen) to suit their whims and caprices, those that are prone to receiving bribes capitalize on that and cheat the whole society. The worst of it all is that society looks on for such scrupulous people to cheat massively that they tend to be revered in the society for the wealth that is illegally acquired. What signal does such a societal (unchecked bribery and corruption) crime give to other civil servants and/or people that are also aspired to get easy money?

Yes, many would attempt to pay bribes in order to get jobs at ministries or those areas within the civil service where the civil servant and the public interface are intense. For example, a civil servant may interact with a lot of people who need to ship or collect goods and cargos from the country's harbours; here the people in need would have to face some 'hungry and bribe-taking' custom officers. Another area of shame is where people make a living on taking bribes before issuing common travelling passport to a citizen of Ghana, when the officer knows that the citizen has the basic right to own a passport without any hindrance whatsoever. Why has such an act of shame persisted in Ghana for so long a time? When I was preparing to travel to the Diaspora, for the first time, in the later part of the 1970s, the so called passport deals, a negative connotation signifying bribery, was at its greatest height. Today in the 21st century the same anti-societal activity is going on. This has drawn many able-bodied young people and even some who are 'well-advanced' in age into the street of Accra to join the 'connection sector', helping people to get passport for a fee. And there are some people, civil servants, in the passport office that are collaborating with those outside contractors, a lucrative business what? And as said before, those civil servants that have turned the organization into their 'private cocoa farms' and nakedly robbing the poor innocent citizen in need have anonymity; they are there until their pension time, if nothing drastic happens to warrant their removal from office.

Anybody who has ever brought applications to the branches of the ministry of land to effect the transfer of land ownership from one person to another would bear me out how certain unscrupulous civil servants delay processing the application and thereby creating "strategic windows" for corrupt officials to collect bribes before one could get the help being sought after. It would take a number of years and some 'underground payments' before applications, which ought to have taken barely days or at most two weeks to process, could be finalised. Why can't the ministry of land make the application forms for the transfer of ownership of land (from the seller to the buyer) available to the applicants? The application forms must be easy and comprehensive to fill, opening no room to individual interpretations and unnecessary delays. And above all, there must be a dateline at which application forms, that have been filled in and submitted to the authorities, be processed and confirmation and/or the transfer of the ownership accepted by the authorities or not. Whether the application forms submitted to the land officials would go to some chiefs, the custodians of lands in our traditional sense, to witness the transfer or not that should not be the task of the applicants. What is of importance to the applicants in particular and to the society in general is to instill the principle of 'just in time delivery' of service to the public.

If the society wants to safeguard against waste of time (a very scarce resource for many productive and busy people), bribery and corruption, applicants should be attended to at just one point. Just as it is in serious businesses, an effective company would encourage a customer to do most of his or her business with the company just at one point of contact. Thus, the customer buys, for example, a very complex, sophisticated and expensive good or product (e.g. a car or a house) at one point. All arrangements for the payment, insurance to cover the possession and the use of the good, some accessories and the after sales services would be taken care of by the company.

If the buyer agrees to the terms of trade as discussed by both parties, the representative of the selling company and the buyer then sign for the agreement. The company representative will, in turn, send the various information to all departments (within the firm) and to some alliance partners (e.g. insurance company and logistic firms) to solicit for their co-operation in co-ordinating and/or integrating their respective resources and activities that would help deliver value and satisfaction to the buyer, all in accordance with the promises given to the customer. One might think that private firms alone work as discussed above, but this is not true. In serious societies, civil servants are trained and supported, but controlled also, to deliver value and satisfaction to clients that come to them with their problems. It is from the tax payments of the client and many others that the civil servant gets paid. Every client therefore should be seen as an important asset and not as a liability as many civil servants perceive them to be.

The discussion about the behaviour of some civil servants in Ghanaian institutions has gone on unchecked for years. In the year 2005 one reads about an ex-president of Ghana, someone who ruled the country for over 20 years, getting so crossed about the massive corruption and bribery in Ghana. This ex-president just left office in the year 2000. This social evil is perceived to have reached its peak; it has been there for a very long time. How on earth could some people, within the education service and some other ministries, have ghost names on their pay rolls for a long time? The answer lies in the fact that many people aid and abet with them. If someone is cheating the public it is alright. "Obiara didi wo nadwuma ho" ('everyone benefits from his or her work"). Some of the headlines in the Ghanaian news papers, in the 21st century highlight the massive bribery and corruption within the Ghanaian judiciary too. It appears that there is no public service organisation that comes clean from the public contempt because of the prevalence of the increase in bribery and corruption. Taken together, Ghana would have revolutions upon revolutions and governments upon governments, the civil service that is there to implement government policies and to serve the

Understanding Things As They Are In Ghana

people, needs be overhauled, if Ghana can make any headway in its development. It is not surprising that some people have claimed that Ghanaians are all magicians. How can people living under such harsh conditions, most of which are purely man-made, cope with it all? This brings me to the discussion of my encounters with some private individuals both in Ghana and in the Diaspora.

3

My Encounter with Fellow Ghanaians, In The Diaspora and In Ghana

Sitting In the Same Sinking Boat but With Common and Divergent Interests

Here, I first start to discuss my encounter with some people, all from my little home town in Ghana, Nyinahin (popularly known as 'New York'). I knew the people very well in Ghana before we met each other in the Diaspora. Between the latter part of the 1970s and the latter part of the 1980s, there were about 30 people from my little town in Ghana, all living in Hamburg alone, in the then West Germany. There were others from the same little town that lived in Hanover, Düsseldorf, Bremen and Karlsruhe, all in the then West Germany. We had come to Germany at different times, but we fell on each other to build some kind of a social network. We had so closed social interactions that the bond that existed between us made it possible to spread information among us about developments at home (Ghana, especially in our little town), information about who else had come newly (from our little town in Ghana) to join us in the Diaspora. Information also spread among us about what each person had come to Germany, for example, to do and the possibilities and problems facing us. What was common with us all, those that had

My Encounter With Fellow Ghanaians

left our little town in Ghana to come to Germany, England, USA, Canada, Italy, and Holland, for example, was the drive to leave the hard conditions that prevailed in our dear Ghana in general and our little town in particular behind us.

Already in the latter part of the 1970s many young people, like young people from other areas, left our little town for Europe in search for better opportunities to realize our potentialities, for Ghana was not offering that chance. This vision that all of us had, made us pursue individual strategies, which we hoped would make each and every one of us see the vision become a reality. Some invested their time and energy in working, right from the day one, to acquire some wealth that would enable them return to Ghana or to our little town to do some gainful investments. Some of us took to education, a long investment option that took much time to bear fruits. What was not apparent to many of us was the time horizon that was appropriate for any of us to realize his or her vision and/or goal so that a decision could be taken to return to Ghana and get re-integrated. The pursuit of the various visions and/or goals for many of us was not without problems. A stable stay and acquisition of working permit and of job in the Diaspora, for example, were real hurdles for many of us to jump over before any vision or goal can be realized. For some, the situation regarding the stability and the acquisition of the relevant staying documents were a nightmare. Yet returning to Ghana was an option no one from us voluntarily would choose. Many had lost hope in Ghana, a long time ago, so a return to Ghana could only come on when there was something substantial to take along, else one would fight on with the immigration authorities for a stay and the possibility to work or study; no matter what it took, many were not going to go back just empty handed, no wealth no higher education.

It is not difficult for any reader to understand the type of behaviour and the struggle of some 50 young people (In Hamburg, Hanover, Düsseldorf, Bremen), all from one village, being depicted here, when one relates their plight to their background characteristics (the numerous problems in Ghana discussed above). Because of my close social interactions with my 'townspeople' I knew much more about the possibilities and the constraints we all faced. There were other Ghanaians, about 1000 in Hamburg alone also sharing the same possibilities and constraints with my 'townspeople' and me, a subject I will return to later on. Realizing our common as well as our individual interests and problems, my 'townspeople' intensified our social contacts at very regular intervals. We met to share meals and exchange experiences and information. Through such meetings new arrivals from our town (in Ghana), that might have had nowhere to live in Hamburg, for example, were put up by someone, an 'old comer'; the 'new comer' would also be helped to go about securing the right staying permits and whatever, until such time that the person would be able to manage the situation all by himself or herself. A typical example is that a new arrival could be helped to get a job, even if it demanded that someone among us, the 'old comers' would have to risk by giving a 'new comer' the former's working permit. It was an impersonation so it was not treated light when discovered by the German migration authorities. Yet most of us took that risk.

We, from my little town, had a share of mind that we were all sitting in a sinking boat; we need to hold each other and let our thoughts and efforts converge so that we could survive some imminent catastrophe. It wasn't a pleasant thing to have failed to secure one's stay in Germany and been deported with empty hands. Relatives, friends, acquaintances and some people in our little town would not understand and sympathize with a deportee, more especially when the deportee had come from the Diaspora with nothing. The deportee would not only be seen as a failure, he or she would be subjected to constant ridicule by many people. This is because one's failure is compared to those that have succeeded to stay in Germany to achieve their goals.

Imagining that about more than 50 young people, from a little town with about 2000 inhabitants at the time, left a rural village for the Diaspora, the village would feel the impact. Most of us were in our early twenties when we first came to Germany. Besides the 50 young people that made their way to Germany there were several others, from the same village, that also made their way to other areas, predominantly to England, USA, and Canada. In the latter part of the 1970s throughout to the present time, there has been active and massive support, on the part of families that have the means, to bring their children to anywhere in the Diaspora. This has been the reaction of the people to the overall miserable conditions, under which they live. We all, the hundreds of us that have left one village, have village background, something that was and is an opportunity for the aged population to hand over their farms and/or activities in the village to our generation. Yet, no one seems to have any hope in the farming and other activities undertaken in the village so they would go at any length to get their children and/or younger relatives to travel abroad in search for some hope and fortune. This reaction to harsh economic conditions, as discussed elsewhere in this paper, is not unique to my village people or other people in Ghana who have also done everything they could to help their children or relatives travel to the Diaspora. The world has seen mass exodus of people of all walks of life, running from poverty, misery and persecution, at different times in the history of mankind.

Probably what makes the situation of my 'townspeople', the Diasporas under discussion here, is the little or no improvement in the living standards of those we are expected to help, back at home in Ghana, while we are living in affluence in the Diaspora. Each and every one of us, in the Diaspora, belongs to a family. The family members expect that some kind of a multiplier effect of our presence in the Diaspora must occur. The popular saying is that "if the family helps you to travel to the Diaspora, you would also have to help to bring one or two people or more to the Diaspora. Those helped by you would also have to help other members in the family to travel to the Diaspora". In the end, one finds that if such a familiar agreement were to be realizable and/or workable, there would be no one, especially young people, left in our village. Similar social 'agreement' has been reached with almost all Ghanaians now living in the Diaspora. Only a few, those from families with strong material wealth, might send their children to the Diaspora probably just to encourage them to pursue some kind of education or learn some trade and encouraged to return home as soon as that mission is accomplished. For the majority of us, your 'value' and or 'importance', in the eyes of the numerous family members (we have extended families), is measured in how many people you have helped, financially and/or by other means, to travel to the Diaspora. In addition to that, one is also expected to help provide a roof over the head for the family members, some of which would be having no where to lay their heads. These expectations produced some attitudes and behaviours in many of us in the Diaspora, some very positive but others very negative. I explore these attitudes and behaviours below.

In the course of time, the little social network that consisted of my 'townspeople' became a bridge for many of us to establish relationships with other people and/or other groups of people from Ghana. At work places (mostly cleaning and washing plates), one could easily meet other Ghanaians, not from one's own home town but from other parts of Ghana, and friendship was established. At some occasions one would bounce into a former schoolmate, who had also come to struggle in the Diaspora, and friendship would start from there. All in all there were a lot of young men and women, besides my townspeople, from Ghana that had all come to live in Hamburg, in our 1000s. Strange in enough, all of us shared one big thing in common. Thus, one's major goal was to do the most he or she could to better his/her living conditions in the Diaspora and to also help improve upon the living conditions of the relatives one had left behind, in Ghana. Unfortunately, people started to have some strange attitude towards money and the means to earn that. For some people the insatiable attitude towards money made them behave inhumanly towards their fellow Ghanaians, although under the pretence of friendship, brotherhood and sisterhood. Yes, over time, many people forgot about the fact that we sat in the same sinking boat. Some started to put their personal interests and/or success over and above others' interests. Many even went to the extent of pursuing their personal interests and goals at the cost of fellow Ghanaians.

The series of the social networks, to which many Ghanaians belonged, became the venue for most of us to compare our respective performances with each other. The performance was about, for instance, the number of people (from one's family) one had helped to get to the Diaspora, the help to put up a house for the family in Ghana, the help to give someone in the family some capital for investments in some income-bringing activities and the help to constantly remit money or ship some material things to the family members in Ghana. With the close ties that existed between members of the various social networks, information spread quickly to all about what each and every one of us was doing for the family back home in Ghana. One's family members in Ghana would also compare the performance of a family member in the Diaspora with that of anyone they also know to be living in the Diaspora. One would hear comparisons such as "this person has been in the Diaspora for only two or three years, but has been able to bring two or three relatives to the Diaspora. Or that someone has sent cars, trucks and some containers full of things, all within a short period of time that the person was domiciled in the Diaspora". The strange thing about such comparisons was that how some people quickly earned money in such magnitude, which enabled them to offer massive help to their family members was not something many people bothered to ponder over. For some people, the attitude towards acquisition of wealth, no matter what means under which the person made that, was at play here. Whether someone engaged in prostitution, drug trafficking, smuggling fellow Ghanaians to the Diaspora for fees and stealing, for example, were of less importance to many people.

Especially in Germany, the immigration laws were very strict during the 1970s and 80s. It was not easy at all for someone to acquire the requisite legal permits to stay and to work. The same could be said about to stay and to study, if one did not come to the country with a study visa. The battle to get the legal documents was a nightmare for many. There were a number of options to obtain the legal permits, but each demanded tough conditions to be met. For example, to get a study visa, which would enable one to live in the country for some time without getting into trouble with the country's immigration laws, one had to really study. All those who secured their stay by the enjoyment of the student visa would have to constantly prove that they were studying and making progress with the study, else one's stay permits would be terminated and the consequences could be a deportation. So here one would imagine the stress that those who committed themselves into studying would have. Students had not enough time to work and earn money so that they could send substantial help to the family members in Ghana. Family members in Ghana had no understanding for why a relative in the Diaspora would waste his or her time to study, knowing very well that many in Ghana are waiting for some help to come from him or her. Although education is a long-term investment, many relatives had no patience to wait for some returns that would only surface in the remote future for them. Many are short-term oriented so they expect that quick help should flow to them, else one would not earn their respect and some would not even want to have anything to do with you any more.

For many a students at that time, the social pressures from family members in Ghana to help them, in general, and the pressure from one's peers in the Diaspora (those selling it all to others that they have done this and that for their relatives) caused them to give up the pursuit of education. Many talented young people became victims to the quick search for wealth; they gave up their studies.

Two examples are provided here to illustrate how some students started to behave strangely, giving up their studies and joining the people who scrambled for money, no matter the means. One student at the "Fachhochschüle" (a kind of Technical University) went into the so called "buying and selling business". He managed, at the start, to collect money from close friends, under the pretext that he was travelling to Ghana and would help anybody who would like to bring money to some relatives at home or would want the money to be put at one's bank account in Ghana. I was one of the victims that gave money to this person. He was supposed to deposit the money into my account; because of that I gave him even my Ghanaian bank book. This person was a close friend of mine so I had no doubt in my mind that my money would be used by him. This student who had turned a business person over night knew many people so he managed to collect a lot of money, with the promise that he was going to help us all bring our money safely home (to Ghana). Ghanaians, at the time, were facing major difficulties in remitting people in Ghana; one could not trust the banking system in Ghana then.

In the early 1980s, the Ghanaian banks broke their oath to withhold the clients' accounts to outsiders, an individual or a government authority. Banks disclosed information about clients' bank deposits to a government that was in to just punish the so called rich people, as many believed. The government issued an ultimatum to people that had bank deposits that exceeded 50,000. Ghanaian cedis to come forward to explain how they came by that amount or else their money would be confiscated. Certainly, in an economy where the informal sector, for example, is dominated by illiterates, where there is no mandatory gazette that all business transactions be documented and where there is no clear policy that all businesses should have some book-keeping and accounting records for inspection, when need be, such a sporadic counter-productive measure did more harm than good. It could happen that many 'bribe takers' and corrupt people had deposited huge sums of money at the banks but to have asked everyone, including those that had no knowledge and/or possibility to document what they spent on and earned from their businesses because they were illiterates and there were no proper socio-economic infrastructure to enhance that accountability, was a very ill-thought measure a government could think of. The aftermath of such a counter-productive measure was that many people lost trust in the banks; the thieves, the corrupt ones and the innocent ones all opted to save their money somewhere or transact their monetary exchanges through private individuals.

This brings us back to the behaviour of the 'student businessman' that was given money by many people in the Diaspora. With the help of some people's money and, of course his own money, 'the student businessman' bought and shipped about two or three containers full of merchandise to Ghana. He flew to Ghana so all those that had given the 'student businessman' money expected and trusted that their respective monies would be sent to the recipients (to make some bank deposits or to give money to some specific people personally). No sooner than the 'student businessman' arrived in Ghana, many rang their relatives and told them to go to the 'student businessman' to collect money sent for them. When many approached the 'student businessman' it turned out that he had used some people's money, without their consent, as a capital to buy some merchandise to be sold in the Ghanaian marketplace. Wasn't that a fraudulent behaviour? Wasn't that a major blow to the trust that people had in him and also in many other people too? For here was a person, from whom no one would expect such a behaviour. The consequence for the 'student businessman' was that he ran into debts, here and there; and the business in Ghana too did not flourish.

Some say that people in Ghana who were expected to help the 'student businessman' sell his merchandise and manage his other investments disappointed him. Eventually, he gave up the education entirely. He also could not continue the "buying and selling business" because he had no capital to do that any more, after many would not want to give money to him again. In the long run he had to chase new staying permit status because he had lost the student status. He had to pay massive money for the "paper marriage" and he ended up going into the "taxi-driving" business.

The other example was also about a student who also, overnight, turned to be a businessman. He was a student at the Hamburg University. At some point in time, the student was visiting Ghana, almost three four times a year. Again, he too was able to collect money from innocent Ghanaians that were undergoing hardships (remember that many had no staying permits and had to hide themselves and wealth from the authorities) with the promise to bring his 'clients' money to Ghana safely. For some time he succeeded to bring money to where the monies were intended to go. For many other times people's money locked up in his "invisible businesses". Problems started to heap up on the student businessman. He had virtually given up studies. He was riding in a Mercedes Benz car, not new of course, but he was making a personal statement that he had succeeded by riding in that car. He became the 'talk of the town'. All who knew him thought that he was successful. The school did not give him anything, but the business did. However, in the course of time, rumours had it that he even went into drug business. He was getting 'damned rich' and was becoming more and more popular in the eyes of those who would not ponder over things, but just admire wealth no matter how that came about. When students gave up their studies and entered into all sorts of dubious activities to make money, people that were also after quick money did match their destinies with such 'heroes', if I should call them so. But like the first 'student businessman's example above, the second student that also became 'damned rich' all of a sudden became poor and had many debts hanging around the neck. One day, to our shock, news came to many Ghanaians in Hamburg that a former student had attempted a suicide at a railway station. He threw himself at an in-coming train, wanting to die. He did not die, fortunately, but lost all of his two legs. His two legs were amputated. He is now a handicapped person. The two student examples provided here are just the tips of an iceberg, when trying to discuss the attitude and the behaviour that many fellow Ghanaians exhibited in Germany, while struggling to improve upon one's life and those of relatives at home (Ghana).

In the quest for quick money, some young women and men from Ghana entered into the prostitution and the 'peep show' industry. Even if prostitution is not a foreign phenomenon to a Ghanaian, there is some kind of such an activity also in Ghana, the way some Ghanaians plunged into the prostitution and the 'peep show' (something very foreign to a Ghanaian) was alarming. They were lured into such an industry with 'big money'. What most of the people that entered into the industry in question did not know was what price they were going to pay in the long-run for having gone to work in the industry. Rumours have it that the men and women that were engaged in the "peep show" business were drugged to have life sex on stage, where people came to watch them perform sexual acts. Imagine someone under the influence of drugs having sex before 100s of people one does not know. Drugs made them perform abnormally long hours, to the joy and pleasure of the paid spectators, but the actors and actresses were damaging their bodies. At most many that went into the 'peep show' business and did have sex under the influence of drugs, especially the men, were reported to have lost their manhood after a few years. If between the ages of 25 and 35 a Ghanaian man loses his manhood, the person would never be happy again in mingling with other fellow Ghanaians. This is because people gossip a lot about someone's behaviour and/or problems; some would even see a problem such as the one depicted here as a punishment for engaging in an activity, which one was/is not supposed to undertake.

For some women that went into the 'peep show' business, they were not only drugged to have sex on stage, but were also filmed. Pornographic films, with some Ghanaian women in action, were a shock to many Ghanaians in the early 1980s. This prompted many people to look for such films to buy and to help their diffusion among the Ghanaian community; yes gossip and condemnation set in. Many Ghanaians could not see, what the hell would propel a fellow Ghanaian woman to disgrace herself, her relatives and Ghanaians, by having sex before 100s of people and allowing that to be filmed and commercialised. But that was the hard evidence of the 'craze' for quick and big money to help oneself and the relatives at home. Someone bought some of the pornographic films in which one Ghanaian woman participated, and brought it to the woman's mother at home (in Ghana). The person was from the same village as the 'pornographic star' so he/she felt ashamed and disgraced by the act of a fellow townsperson. Many Ghanaians in Germany, at the time, were teasing and blaming him/her, for the conduct of a fellow townsperson, for which he/she had no control. The pornographic film that was sent to the mother of the Ghanaian woman in the film had a very sad effect on the poor mother. Although the poor mother was getting regular remittances and help from her daughter, she never knew or suspected that her daughter would be engaging in such a 'dirty activity, as many saw it at the time and perhaps even now. The poor mother of the 'pornographic star was believed to have collapsed on seeing the film, just from the beginning and discovering that it was her daughter many people had been talking about concerning 'bad means' to acquire wealth. This rumour was going on in her village but the poor woman did not know anything about that, until the film revealed that the rumour about using 'bad means' to acquire wealth was about her own daughter she had loved and admired over the years for her excellent performance in the Diaspora. The strange attitude and behaviour among Ghanaians do not end here. Below are also a few other accounts.

Several other 'gangs', not students, sprang up as businesswomen and businessmen loading and shipping containers upon containers to Ghana. There was nothing wrong with that if such business people had gone the genuine way. Many country women and men were deceived to believe that they could trust some fellow Ghanaian business people. It was about transferring money to Ghana through some business people. Many Ghanaian reposed their trust and confidence that their hard-won wealth could reach home, Ghana, if given to a Ghanaian business woman or man. But many proved to be

My Encounter With Fellow Ghanaians

greedy and fraudulent business people that were very indifferent to the sufferings many fellow Ghanaians were going through in Germany at the time. Knowing that it was difficult for many Ghanaians to save at the German banks and/or have money on them, because they could be arrested by the police and deported outright, a fellow Ghanaian business person became the last resort to trust. A few business people proved very honest and trustworthy so it was difficult to distinguish between the bad business people from the good ones, until one got his or her fingers burnt in the act of trusting a Ghanaian business person and giving a huge sum of money to him or her. This reminds me of the tragic death of a schoolmate of mine at the Kotoka International Airport. The fellow I am talking about was at the same secondary school, my classmate, during the first three years, after which time he left for another school to complete the secondary education. It was a glad scene when other classmates of mine met the deceased classmate of ours in Hamburg. We visited each other on a number of occasions in Hamburg. One day he felt sick and was diagnosed to have had some kind of a deadly disease. The German authorities, being so generous, gave my late classmate a staying permit because of humanitarian reasons. The doctors of my classmate advised him not to return to Ghana, without the consent of the doctors. This was because the doctors were sure that his presence in Ghana without being entrusted into a special doctor's care could result in his, my classmate's, death. What a predicament! My classmate, like many of us, wanted to do something for the relatives at home in Ghana so he gave money to someone, a Ghanaian business person or a friend that left Hamburg for Ghana. My classmate wanted the person, to whom he gave the money, to invest in some project for him. So many days, weeks, and months elapsed and no news came from Ghana to tell my classmate about what had become of the project, for which money had been given to someone.

At last, my classmate, the sick person, could not bear it any more; he decided to travel to Ghana, defying doctors' advice not to travel to Ghana without their knowledge. My classmate wanted to see his project and/or to see the person to whom he gave his money. He took along some medicines with him, hoping that he could survive within some few days in Ghana, after which he might return to

Hamburg. Having been away for a little while, my classmate arranged for some relatives to meet him at the Kotoka International Airport. My classmate landed, passed through the Ghanaian Immigration and came out to meet relatives that had come to the airport to meet him. Being very anxious and curious to know what had become of his money, sent through someone from Hamburg, he asked the relatives, which had come to meet him, about his project. The answer my classmate had was that there had not been any project that was supposed to be his; if there was such a project at all they, the relatives, knew nothing about that. The next question my classmate was said to have asked was the whereabouts of the person to whom he gave his money. He learned to his bewilderment that the person in question had already left Ghana again for the Diaspora. Where in the Diaspora the fraudulent person had gone to, nobody could tell my classmate. On hearing that news, my classmate collapsed instantly at the airport and that was the end of his short life; he was between 25 and 29 years. He never went home to meet his mother and father and siblings who might have been so glad to see him, whether or not he had brought with him something from the Diaspora. Why and how could someone that knew the plight of my late classmate defraud him like that? The answer is not distant to find. Somewhere in this book attempt has been made to discuss how some people in Ghana had always sought to exploit the needy in Ghana. It could be about a young school lever seeking a job in our civil service or even in some private businesses, a potential traveller applying for a common passport or a travel visa, a potential business person seeking licence, and so on. The list can be too long. There are people who want quick money so they would subject innocent people in need to some untold frustrations, until some 'under the table payments are made', before the red tapes hindering a person from achieving his or her goals would be removed. And this attitude and/or behaviour accompanied many Ghanaians into the Diaspora. They never thought about and sympathised with Ghanaians that had to go through hell before securing some legal documents, if lucky. Below are some accounts of the ordeals many had to go through, especially in Germany during the 1970s and the 1980s.

Going Through Some Ordeals

In German, during the 1970s and the 1980s especially, what counted most, for many Ghanaians, was to secure some jobs. Often times one could not satisfy himself or herself with only one or two jobs, the jobs have to be more than one. Since many Ghanaians at the time did not have high qualifications that would get them well-paid jobs, they had to do several jobs to get money for their own up-keep and for the family members in Ghana. It was not uncommon to observe that many Ghanaians had little sleep and time to eat properly. This was because some people were always on the run after jobs or from one job to the other. The irony of it all was that Germany was not a place to harbour economic immigrants. So many Ghanaians, including my 'townspeople', had to find other means to secure their stay in Germany. I have already mentioned that to study would accord someone a legal permit to study and even, to some extent, to work. The other means, especially during the 1970s and the 80s, for many Ghanaians were, for example, to seek a political asylum and also to get married to a German citizen.

It was not easy at all, for someone from Ghana at the time, to acquire an asylum status; one out of twenty got that status. Already in the mid of the 1980s 1000s of Ghanaians had come to stay in Germany and many opted for the asylum status. That appeared to be somewhat easy, compared to the other options, to acquire. Even majority of the asylum applications were rejected, many gained time to work and to amass some wealth, while the immigration office investigated and eventually decided on their case. For many Ghanaians, at the time, asylum seeking provided the chance to quickly get into the labour market. Asylum seekers, for sometime past, could be granted working permit, while awaiting decision on the asylum application. This measure fitted perfectly into the objectives of many Ghanaians then; they were in Germany to quickly get rich so that they could return to Ghana, if their asylum applications were rejected.

The other option to secure one's stay in Germany was to get married to a German citizen. This last choice was very expensive, especially for those that entered into "paper marriages". Some Germans exploited the situation of the Ghanaians who were in desperate need of legal permits to stay. And here, some Ghanaians and other Africans collaborated with some Germans to exploit those who needed marriage to secure their stay. Paid marriages came to dominate the scene. Many Ghanaians, for example, facing immigration problems at the time, paid huge sums of money to some Germans and the middlemen who helped them with the marriage. Another strange behaviour, among some Ghanaians, was that they capitalize on the fellow Ghanaians' problem with the acquisition of legal staying permits. A market emerged for some people who were described as "connection people". Yes, they could help a fellow country man or woman to get a German citizen to marry or could even offer to help someone write his or her asylum application, all for a fee. Here we were with the same attitude and behaviour that some unscrupulous people in Ghana have been putting up over the years. Some did not want to go to the German factories to work or to offices to clean and or to restaurants to wash plates, as many of their fellow Africans were doing, they wanted to get to easy money. Arranging marriages and helping people to write asylum applications earned them money.

The plight of many Ghanaians during the 1980s in West Germany was very miserable, although the people were at the same time making money. Plight in the sense that most applications submitted for political asylum status were rejected very often. It was not pleasant to watch many Ghanaians that had to live from week to week, with just a week's staying permit. That meant that they had to report at the immigration office almost every week to find out what had become of their application for the political asylum status. Some might end up in the hope of getting some positive result, a one or two weeks extension of one's staying permit. Others might end up with negative result. Frequent visits to lawyers, many lawyers profited from the poor applicants, to get help in their struggle for asylum status led to large sums of money running out of the pockets of people that were doing tedious manual works, sometimes one or two, before they could make ends meet. Many had to report frequently to the immigration offices, some of whom would, during such visits, never return to their homes. Their asylum applications were rejected so the police would be brought in to take them away from the immigration office. The next thing a person , arrested by the police at the immigration office, would see is a march to where he or she was living in Hamburg or any other part in Germany, with the police, and a search would be conducted in the person's apartment by the police. The person would be deported after a search in his or her apartment. If the search resulted in the police finding some money, they took that to finance the deportation; or whatever the money was used for could be anyone's guess.

With the ordeals that faced many Ghanaians, living from one day to another day was full of high uncertainty. All this made many people intensify their search for jobs and doing many jobs, where they made sure that their hard-won monies were kept not in the bank or by themselves, but by someone they could trust. 'Someone one could trust' became not only the person to confide one's secrets in, but also everything (a bank, liaison between him/her and lawyers, etc). Here, some Ghanaians actually fulfilled that function and helped those in need. However, there were others who belied their intentions to the needy and promised to help, but in the final analysis monies or some valuable things entrusted into their care were never returned to their true owners, more especially when the victims had been deported. The case reported about my classmate that died at the Kotoka airport, on hearing that a person he trusted had defrauded him is a case in point. Since it was not easy to contract a genuine marriage with a German citizen or to acquire a student status, because they all demanded that certain conditions be fulfilled, many Ghanaians were left with no choice but to go for the asylum option. To those who succeeded to win time, because the decision to reject their asylum application took some years, were able to work and save towards their return to Ghana or leave Germany for some other countries, should the 'D-Day' arrive; thus, the day their applications would be rejected and would be asked to leave the country.

Out of Frustration or What?

In the struggle to grab every opportunity that came in the way of many, desperate and some criminal people, at the time, some German companies that sought to help customers to buy goods on credit basis were defrauded. For many Ghanaians, it was a shock to hear that some fellow Ghanaians had contacted catalogue and post order firms to buy huge amounts of goods, all on credit. Although the companies were going to get, hopefully, their money paid in some future time, it was a tremendous help to many customers to be able to buy several goods that were very expensive and technologically complex at the time. Examples of such goods were deep freezers, refrigerators, musical instruments (stereos), colour televisions, video recorders, sewing machines, and vacuum cleaners; you name them. The firms would bring such goods to the customer's door post, what a service! For most Ghanaians at the time, these services (credit payment, delivery on time and delivery at one's door step) were an innovative thing, seen from our Ghanaian perspective at the time. I don't think we have companies in Ghana today, in the 21 century, which provide the   services or solutions mentioned above. But many Ghanaians abused such generous problem-solving ability of the German companies, all for the achievement of their own personal interests.

For the lack of long-term orientation and of respect for others' interests, many desperate and criminal persons (some were real criminals) ordered several goods from several catalogue and post order firms. Some could get containers full of goods ordered, but unpaid for, and shipped them to Ghana. The people that shipped goods that they had not paid and were not going to pay also left Germany for Ghana for good, perhaps. After some time when the catalogue and the post order firms were not getting the expected regular flow of payments of goods sold to some Ghanaians, after several reminders and/or warnings, the case was reported to the police. Immigration authorities were also contacted about the fraudulent act of some Ghanaians. So the police, the immigration authorities and the firms combined to hunt the culprits and to also do all they could to prevent such an act to happen again. Some local papers started to write headlines about some Ghanaian syndicate that had duped some German firms. Some of the people that indulged in those fraudulent acts asserted that it was one of the means to get 'our balance' from what the colonialists stole from Africans. Could you believe that? Was that individual theft a means to compensate for what the colonialists are believed to have stolen from Africa? If one could see how most of the resources from Africa and many other areas that underwent colonialism were sent to develop the countries of the colonialists, then, such a perception of some Ghanaians was not only childish, but also senseless looking at things from a development point of view. While the colonialists owned and controlled all critical resources in their colonies, a Ghanaian that became a labourer and/or an economic slave in the Diaspora thought that stealing petty things like deep freezers and TV sets was a way of getting back the resources that were stolen from Africa. These thefts were exposed and eliminated, at no distant time. What impact did such malpractices of some Ghanaians in Germany have on Ghana then? The positive impact was virtually zero; such acts could not help uplift the development of the country. The negative impact, as accounted for below, was tremendous.

The image of Ghana and Ghanaians that lived in Germany became summarily tarnished. Doing business with a Ghanaian at the time was a risky thing and, hence, credit sales for example had to be restricted, if not completely be out of question. Yes, those who thought that they were smart did not think about the impact of such silly act for the long time to come on many innocent Ghanaians. It also affected other customers, especially those with foreign background, when doing business with German firms. For some time, one had to only be in the position to pay for everything in cash. Many people at the time did just manual work for meagre payment (s). To buy expensive goods such as modern colour TV sets or a Video recorder and musical instrument (Stereo), things that most of us highly aspired to possess during the time, was very expensive. Could such shorted-sighted behaviour be attributed to the 'burden', which many of us believed to have been bearing? It was difficult to understand why some people would go that far to behave the way they did, thus shipping containers full of unpaid goods to Ghana. Many Ghanaians, over the years, have had the urge to fulfil the 'family agreements' they have once made; some would take whatever means it took (see the example above) to get their hands on material things that could be sent to Ghana for own use and for some relatives.

Ordeals or Not, Family Agreements Must Be Fulfilled

In spite of some of the ordeals discussed above, many continued to help bring other relatives to face similar tragedies and/or opportunities. Why would someone want a relative to come and face similar hardships? No, it wasn't that people were callous and would want their brothers and sisters to also face some untold hardships in the Diaspora. The perception of help was and/is different among many Ghanaians. Many Ghanaians believed and still do believe that every person has his or her own luck. "Nsa nyinaa nye pe ("all the human fingers are not the same"). That is to say, some people would be lucky enough to quickly get the necessary permits to stay and to work. As said elsewhere in this book, ability to help a relative to come to stay and struggle in the Diaspora was an important way of measuring a Ghanaian's success in the Diaspora. Such a performance became a popular topic whenever Ghanaians met in small or big circles. Competition set in regarding the ability to help finance someone come to live in the Diaspora. In the fulfilment of the 'family agreement' (not written but informal; it was powerful because it affected behaviour), some people actually were able to finance the travel of some relatives to the Diaspora. I know of a person who was able, already in the middle of the 1980s, to help bring about six or more of her relatives to live in Germany alone, while her spouse was unable to bring a single person from his family to the Diaspora. You could imagine what people were saying about the man for failing to help his relatives at home (Ghana), compared to what his spouse was able to do. The man is still, in the 21 century, unable to bring a relative to live in the Diaspora; he is therefore looked upon as a failure in the eyes of many Ghanaians.

As discussed elsewhere, for many Ghanaians, a relative in the Diaspora must be able to help other relatives to come to live and work in the Diaspora. He or she must also be able to build a house for the extended family or for one's core family (only husband, wife and children) and give some other help to the extended family members. Except one is a Ghanaian (an insider) it would be difficult to

My Encounter With Fellow Ghanaians

imagine how many Ghanaians in the Diaspora feel about, for example, how they are evaluated by some Ghanaians in general and by one's relatives in particular. If you cannot totally break bonds with your relatives, you would never be at peace, until you are able to meet some of the demands that relatives make on you. I, for instance, was still a student when I left no stone unturned, through genuine studies and part-time work, to help finance two relatives of mine to come to live and work in the Diaspora. After schooling and during my first year at work, in the middle of the 1990s, I helped finance six other relatives to come to live and work in the Diaspora.

In the latter part of the 1990s I also helped finance three other relatives to come to the Diaspora to live and to work. If all these relatives were to also fulfil their family agreements, as I have done, I believe there would be no young man and woman in the extended family that cannot be helped to come to live and to work in the Diaspora; that would have produced a multiplier effect. Or if the people were also to remit constantly to other relatives that are left in Ghana, the living conditions of our extended family would have been markedly improved upon. Until now, my relatives are still calling on me for help because the others I have helped to come to live and work in the Diaspora are not helping. Of course, one or two of them are helping but very minimal. They are willing to help but they find it hard themselves to meet their own immediate needs, let alone helping someone else. This brings us to look closely into the discussion of the fact that what works for someone might not work for the other. Again, the perception of the Diaspora as the solution to one's problems and that of the entire family's is quite deceiving and dangerous. People have lost hope in Ghana and what Ghana can offer them; no serious effort is being made by many people to invest one's time and energy, for example, in doing something valuable in Ghana. 'That people should not think about what their country can offer them, but what they can do for their country', as the late President Kennedy was believed to have said to his fellow Americans, does not apply to Ghanaians. And it might be true that Ghanaians do not believe in such a phrase. This is because USA might have the contextual conditions (basic and functional infrastructures) that enable every 'Tom Dick and Hurry' to exploit his or her potentialities to the individual's self-fulfilment and to the benefit of the entire nation. Ghana, as discussed in the earlier preceding chapters, has no favourable conditions under which individuals can genuinely realize their goals in life and in so doing also help develop the country. Going to the Diaspora to live and work would be the dream everybody wants to see realized. No matter what one tells them about the hardships in the Diaspora, which many Ghanaians face, people would not believe that. The popular question one gets, when trying to tell someone about the conditions in the Diaspora for many Ghanaians, is "if the Diaspora is not good why have you been there for all this long and do not intend to return home"? For many people, every person has his or her own 'angel' that guides him/her. "You help me travel to the Diaspora and you would see wonders", one would hear from a relative. This trend was reinforced by some hard facts, as the following quotation portrays.

> *"In 1988, Rawlings could mention the doctors mainly because their absence was easily noticed. With a little effort he would have found out that most graduates of the country's universities with relatives abroad leave, immediately they graduate, to western Europe and America to work as labourers and perform other menial tasks at which they earn better salaries in a week than the highest paid civil servant in two months. The Ghanaian labourer in London at the beginning of 1989 earning £100 a week is taking home the equivalent of 80,000 cedis in Ghana which is the salary of a middle ranking civil servant in six months, or about a quarter of the annual salary of the chief justice of Ghana. In essence it means the labourer in London in a month earns the equivalent of the chief justice's whole year's salary"* (Adjei, M., 1994, pp. 310-311).

Many young Ghanaians also ventured to enter Germany, with the same hope as the one depicted of London above. The trend to help a relative to come to live and work in the Diaspora continued unabated, in spite of the problems that Ghanaians faced in Germany, acquiring the legal staying and working permits, for example. It was not impossible for someone, a newly arrived person from Ghana, to meet a German citizen who really would want to enter into a genuine marriage with the person. With such an opportunity, the German citizen would take the 'fight' with the German Immigration authorities, on behalf of the Ghanaian needing staying and working permits. The German citizen and his or her would-be spouse could even be asked to go to Ghana to marry and thereby apply for the staying and working permits for the Ghanaian. Many Ghanaians and some Germans genuinely followed such procedures. It was also possible for a newly arrived person, from Ghana, to get into some arranged and paid for marriage with a German citizen. A relative (s) that sponsored the person to come to the Diaspora would also be able to foot the expenses incurred in connection with the 'paid marriage arrangement'. This too worked for many people. Others could also go the school way. Some people who did not have the qualification to enter higher institutions, which would guarantee them access to the staying and working permits, could buy or ask for certificates from some people that enabled them to enroll into some institutions. At some point in time a Ghanaian, that got tired and ashamed by such impersonation with school records, reported the case to some German universities. The impersonation case also went to the immigration authorities. This disclosure made many "faked Ghanaian students at German Universities flee in their numbers from Germany because the police was ordered to search for and arrest them.

Turbulent Settlement in the Diaspora

While the Europeans, in the 1800s, had organized way of helping their people to migrate to USA, Canada, Australia and Africa, for example, what the reader has seen so far is that many Ghanaians had and have migrated without any state organization behind that. The difficulties that many had to go through before they could enter and settle down in Germany, for example, have been narrated. In spite of all the efforts that many Ghanaians put in, luck was not on their side; they could not secure their stay in Germany. Many were deported, while others left Germany for other European countries (e.g. Netherlands, England, France, Italy and Belgium). Others made their way to North America (e.g. USA and Canada). What were some of the forces that made many people refuse to return to Ghana, knowing that they had no chance to stay in Germany or in other wealthy areas in the Diaspora? In Germany the means to gain one's staying and working permits became very restricted and controlled in the course of time. In the early 1980s, especially 1983 and 1984, many Ghanaians were deported from Germany. It coincided with the mass deportation of millions of Ghanaians from Nigeria. It was very common to have heard that a Ghanaian was taken away by the police, while he or she was on the way to do some menial work for meagre pay. The surprise arrest also occurred when a person was lured to go to the immigration office to re-new his or her weekly staying permit. The police would be called in to arrest and to deport the person. Some lawyers that had taken money to protect and defend the poor Ghanaians became 'toothless'. They could not help their clients to, at least, get decent notice of the rejection of their application for legal permits and, for that matter, to able to prepare for their eventual deportation to Ghana.

Some Ghanaians were arrested and deported without being able to go home to take some additional clothes and some money they might have hidden somewhere. These hard measures to deter Ghanaians from staying and or perhaps helping other Ghanaians to enter Germany were making life a real hell for many people. Ghanaian marriages, for example, were being destroyed by such measures. This was because a man that had financed his wife to join him in Germany, but all had put in application for the asylum status, could be arrested and deported. The women would, some of them having one or two or even more children, be made to stay and took care of the children alone. The scene was unbearable for many Ghanaians that cared about the plight of the deportees and the wives and children that were left behind in Germany. I, for instance, wrote a three or four page letter to the then Ambassador of German, Hon. Adusei Poku, appealing to him to intervene to rescue Ghanaian marriages. Especially, the children whose parents were separated by force were undergoing some traumatic and/or psychological problems. The Ambassador acted on my appeal, taking my letter with him, and approached the then Minister of the Interior to help bring a stop to such an inhuman immigration measures that proved to be tormenting for children as well. You could imagine the feeling of a child whose father, the protector of the family, was striped off from the family defencelessly and sent away.

Again, rumours had it that even Ghanaians could help the police arrest a Ghanaian man that was staying illegally. The goal was to go for the deportee's wife afterwards. What was driving some Ghanaians to always capitalize on their fellow Ghanaians' problem for their own benefits? The answer was not difficult to find. Having the right permits to stay and to work in Germany, at the time, was also seen as a sign of success by some people. If you had no such security, you better not get into trouble with some people that had secured their stay in Germany.

To discourage a large number of Ghanaians, for example, to use Germany as an economic haven, several Ghanaians that entered the country during the mid 1980s onwards had no luck to get the quick access to the labour market and/or to school. Many asylum applicants, a means that previously gave a quick access to the labour market and/or some huge social welfare money, had to be put into camps, until such time that their applications were approved. And 1 out of 20 got his or her application for an asylum status approved after about two or three years. Imagine that a person who had been helped, with some scarce family resources, to come to Germany had to wait for two or three years in an asylum camp before his or her application was decided upon. Formerly, the two or three year waiting time for the decision to be made on one's application for the asylum status gave the person an automatic work permit. Many utilized that chance to work legally. This bright opportunity was gone for those that entered Germany after the mid 1980s. One could be kept in a camp for almost two years, after which time his or her application would be rejected and forthright deportation would ensue. What a tragedy for many young Ghanaians that never tasted the good things that, what they dreamt about, the Diaspora had in store for them. The average age of most Ghanaians then was 20 years. They could not realize their dreams. Faced with such immigration procedures, many 'asylum camp dwellers' started to take the law into their own hands and put up all sorts of behaviour.

Some of them had to leave their camping places, against the law then, to go to places, especially Hamburg, where they were sure to get some 'black jobs'. It worked for many people. This also produced problems for many people that lived in some big cities in Germany, especially those that had to hide their 'skins' from the immigration authorities and the police because of lack of legal permits. The number of illegal people surged in the big cities so control was also increased against illegal stay. But the Ghanaian hiding from the authorities would have to go to work. This is where some Ghanaians, for want of money or jealousy, betrayed their fellow Ghanaians that lived in Germany illegally at the time. Some people acted as informants to the police, reporting some Ghanaians that had trouble with the immigration office. In short, for many Ghanaians all the efforts that they put in did not help them secure their stay in Germany. Many were deported, while others left Germany for other European countries (e.g. Netherlands, England, France, Italy and Belgium). Others made their way to North America (e.g. USA and Canada).

The notion that Ghanaians or Africans were in Germany, for example, to 'strike the balance' between the exploitation of Africa and the exploitation of Germany, for example, by Africans did not work. Unfortunately, Africans had no such power that would enable them to control and do whatever they want with the critical resources of their host countries. History has it clearly that some European countries – Belgium, England, France, Italy, Portugal, Germany and Spain shared Africa among themselves; the famous term for this act was know as the partition of Africa (1880-11939). Until such time that many African countries broke free from the domination of their colonial countries a British citizen in Gold Coast (now Ghana) or a Belgian in Congo (now Congo Kinshasa and Congo Brazzaville) could make laws and regulations governing how the host country's (the colony) resources should be developed, tapped and used. Almost all Ghanaians or all Africans that I met in the Diaspora (e.g. Germany at the time) had come to live on the periphery of the host country, being told what to do and to take what was offered and not the opposite. This brings the discussion to my encounter with other Africans.

My Encounter with Other Africans in the Diaspora

Ghanaians that I met in Hamburg had much in common with the other Africans that lived in Germany at the time. I met and befriended some Africans from, for example, Nigeria, Côte d'Voire, Sierra Leone, Gambia, Senegal, Mali, Cameroon, Gabon, Guinea, Uganda, Zaire (now Congo Kinshasa), Angola, Ethiopia, Tanzania, Kenya, Rhodesia (now Zimbabwe), Mozambique and South Africa. What the Africans from the aforementioned countries had in common was that almost all had come to the Diaspora (here Germany, for example) with the major goal to pursue our respective interests, to acquire wealth, to study, to escape persecution (e.g. those from Rhodesia, Angola, Uganda and South Africa) and to experience a new world full of any good thing one could imagine under the sun.

For those Africans that ran away from internal political troubles, where living from one day to the other was full of uncertainty because one could be drawn into civil war (e.g. Angola and Mozambique in the 1970s and the early 1980s), acquiring the German legal staying and working permits were less problematic than those that were classified as merely economic refugees. It was also not so much a problem from people that came from the then Rhodesia (now Zimbabwe) Mozambique and South Africa to obtain legal permits that enabled them to live in Germany. These had come from African countries where millions of their fellow Africans were driven to live in Reserves, deplete of most basic social amenities such as better schools, electricity, telephone, good roads, pipe borne water and shopping centres. Many Africans from the then Rhodesia (now Zimbabwe) and South Africa would always talk about the hardships that they lived in and what the people left behind were living in. The White minorities in those countries (Rhodesia and South Africa at the time in question) would not mingle with the Africans. It was impossible for an African to go to the same good school, shopping centre, and swimming pool with a white person. In Rhodesia and South Africa, the Africans, who were and are still in the majority, could no longer tolerate the White minority domination. The Africans got organized and demanded that power be shared equally among all citizens, where a person's colour, race, and background should not be a factor that determines who should rule over the others.

In Rhodesia and South Africa, the White minority could not 'stomach' such a challenge to share power, some 'ring leaders' and many out-spoken people in the African organizations that fought for power sharing were arrested and detained without trial. The famous first black President of South Africa, Mr. Hon. Nelson Mandela, was a phenomenal example. He was imprisoned for over twenty years for leading the African National Congress to demand not only the dismantle of the Apartheid system (a system that discouraged Whites and Africans to have anything in common), but also to let the people, Whites or Africans, choose their own government. That also meant that the Africans were demanding that Africans too must have the universal suffrage. Mass arrest, torture and restricting people to the Townships became unacceptable the world over so pressure was brought to bear on the Apartheid government, especially through the use of economic sanctions, to refrain from suppressing the African majority and reform the system to embrace all South Africans in the running of the country. Until such time that the Apartheid system was overthrown, many South Africans that went to live in exile were accorded legal protection and offered all the support they needed wherever they lived. So those South Africans that I met in Hamburg during the late 1970s and the 1980s were having quiet and stable stay. However, they could not let go their thoughts on their fellow country men and women that still lived in

South Africa under inhuman conditions. Those Africans that had come from the Rhodesia did face something similar to what the Africans in South Africa faced, although the system the White minority used was not that of Apartheid. But African Rhodesians also could not live in areas where social amenities were well developed; they were also living in the Reserves. Naturally, the Africans organized and demanded that the entire people, White or Africans, must be involved in the choosing of the people to rule the country. Many Africans had to flee Rhodesia; for fear that they would be arrested and detained without trial. The present President, Hon Mr. Robert Mugabe, was a political refugee in Ghana for sometime before returning to run for elections and won as the first black President of Rhodesia (in the early 1980s, where the country also changed name to Zimbabwe). Hence, people that had come from Rhodesia to live in Germany had no problems in getting legal permits. When Zimbabwe attained its first African President and its Independence in 1980, many Africans rejoiced very much over that. Many sat in front of the Television broadcast to watch the unforgettable day's celebration; the late legend Bob Marley went to play at Zimbabwe's. He made us all happy and proud.

People from Angola, Mozambique and Uganda were all accepted in Germany at the time, too, because those countries were either in civil war or there were some brutal freedom fighting activities that manifested in 'head on confrontation' with the colonial rulers. However, in Uganda it was a 'bloody' coup d'etat that was staged by Idi Amin. His brutal and tyrannical rule nearly resulted in a civil war. Hence, people from Uganda that had come to live in Germany also were accepted. These Africans that were genuinely accepted as refugees did not, probably, have the same pressure to help bring one or two relatives to come and live in the Diaspora. There was not much they could to bring relatives, in their numbers, to live in the Diaspora. Many of them had come to the Diaspora by the help of the United Nation's refugee settlement arrangement. It was not easy for people to leave the then Rhodesia and South Africa, for example, to travel abroad. Where would they get the passport and the permission to travel outside their countries? But many of us from the other parts of Africa, Ghana, Nigeria, Cote d'Voire, Gambia, Senegal, for example, could travel freely, with visa or not. It was, therefore, not impossible to imagine why people from West Africa, for instance, found it difficult to obtain legal permits.

The struggle for material things was also less pronounced among the people who had come from countries, which the German authorities considered illegible to political refugee status. While many Ghanaians, Nigerians, Gambians and Zairians were loading containers full of merchandise to ship to their countries, People from Rhodesia (now Zimbabwe), South Africa, Angola and Mozambique did not do that. For them 'home was not cool'. How could they ship merchandise home? How could they follow up to collect their merchandise? Or who could collect the merchandise on their behalf? Ghanaians, for example, did not have to answer such questions. Therefore, many were doing more than two jobs to get money for the purchase of goods that could be sent home at regular intervals. Often times Ghanaians, especially those with legal permits and had money, would load containers with cars and so on and would travel to Ghana to collect them. They could also arrange for someone in Ghana to collect the merchandise on their behalf. It became a competition among Ghanaians, for example, to display wealth by that. In the act of being able to compete with others and/or show that one was also successful, many took to all means (legal and illegal) to amass wealth. This type of behaviour was not common at all among the other Africans, whom I became privileged to meet. Many of the other Africans (e.g. from Rhodesia, South Africa, Angola and Mozambique) were not easy to meet and to befriend. They were not many as, for example, Ghanaians who were in their 1000s at the time. I, for instance, met those I refer to here (thus, those that were not easy to meet and to befriend) because I studied with many of them at the same university, Hamburg. Meeting the other Africans and people from West Africa was a rich experience for me. I learned especially about how different backgrounds could affect behaviour. Someone (an African fleeing Apartheid) that had come from South Africa to live in the Diaspora could not think of loading a container full of merchandise to be shipped to the country in the 1970s and 80s. No relative would expect that from him or her either. The same could not be said about a Ghanaian. Recall that the Ghanaian's per-

My Encounter With Other Africans in the Diaspora

formance, for being in the Diaspora, was evaluated, among other things, by his or her display of wealth and/or material things; containers full of merchandise had to flow to Ghana at regular intervals. While my encounter with some other Africans, as narrated above, resulted from the fact that many of them and I studied at the same university at the time, socializing with most of them outside the university walls was very seldom. I knew where many of them lived in Hamburg and they also knew where I lived, but strange enough we could not meet outside the university walls for 'out-of school' beer or whatever. That was why any time we met each other and there was time, especially during lunch time, we sat at length and talked about problems facing our dear continent, the type of leaders in Africa, and the problems we faced in Hamburg. However, there was a family from Zaire (now Congo Kinshasa) that developed very good social relationship with my family. Through the intimate contacts with the Zairian family we learned much from each other, especially about the problems facing Ghanaians as well as Zairians in Hamburg and in Ghana. The Zairian man (also husband and father; he and the wife had two children) and I first met each other at one particular course, mathematics for economists, which we took together at the Hamburg University in the early 1980s. Since then we became good friends. We once lived in the same student's hostel, each with his own one room on different floors. We therefore met each other several times after school. I took him along whenever I visited some Ghanaians to socialize. He also invited me to several other Zairians. With time, we moved from the students' hostel that was accommodating only bachelor students. Our respective wives joined us so we needed much spacious places to live in. Fortunately, we all got accommodations that were for married students in Catholic students' hostel, very near our university too. This enabled us and our respective families have almost daily contacts.

The contact with the Zairian family also helps me draw some parallels between the attitudes towards being in the Diaspora and the type of behaviour that many Ghanaians put up in the realization of their individual goals. Unlike the other Africans (see above) that were seriously considered as legitimate for refugee status, many Zairians were facing the same problems as many Ghanaians; they

As I Journey Along

were classified as 'economic' refugees. Hence the fight for legal permits, through whatever means possible was intensified by many Zairians as well. As discussed before, staying permit could be given for reasons such as pursuing education, having entered into a marriage with a German citizen and having been granted a political asylum. Of course, some foreigners that had legal stay could also be allowed to bring in their wives or husbands. However, this option was not easy at all. At any rate, some Zairians managed to obtain legal permits that enabled them to stay in peace and pursued their goals. Others went through hell, like many Ghanaians did, because they had no convincing grounds, other than economic reasons, to fight for legal staying permit.

The immigration authorities' and the police's hunt for illegal immigrants made several Zairians also go underground and others left for other European countries, notably France and Belgium. In spite of the high uncertainty that many Zairians faced, some of them lost sight of the fact their leaders, especially Mobutu Sesse Sekou, were very much responsible for the economic misery that had driven them (the younger generation) to come and live in the Diaspora, which had not proved to be easy for them either. Mobutu, the leader of the then Zaire, was supposed to be the richest person in the whole of Africa at the time, while the country he led was one of the poorest in Africa. Ironically, Zaire was and is still rich in natural resources more than many other African countries. President Mobutu would prefer to invest the resources of the country in his own personal accounts and/or businesses in Europe instead of investing in Zaire. Rumours have it that he owned several houses in France, USA and have bank accounts with billions of dollars in foreign banks. The average Zairian was living far below the poverty line. It was therefore a strange behaviour on the part of some Zairians to organize to meet Mobutu, during some of his visits in Europe, where they sang and danced for him. By singing and dancing for Mobutu the people were given some 'ridiculous' amount of money. Why would young men and women forget what had driven them to leave their dear country and go to dance before the person who had been one of the architects responsible for their suffering? It was all about money. Many were pursuing their individual selfish goals at the peril of the entire Zairian nation. This was because by aiding and abetting with the corrupt leader, the former felt that his underdevelopment of the nation by siphoning its resources and depositing them in other countries, he still had the loyalty of the people. Why would the younger generation forget that Mobutu himself, when he was young, felt very dissatisfied with the conditions his people lived in so he staged a military coup? But the modern youngsters did not see the need to fight; to tell Mobutu in the face, when they had chance, that he should go to hell with his 'dubious' riches. They were going to free their country from his grips. Nevertheless, there were Zairians, especially my friend with whom I had had long and stable contacts, who were very critical about the behaviour of their fellow country men and women that sang and danced for Mobutu each time the latter visited some countries in the Diaspora.

On the behaviour of some Zairians discussed above, the Ghanaians I met in Hamburg differed a lot. I remember that in the late 1970s, Ghanaians in Hamburg demonstrated against military rule in Ghana. I was among these demonstrators so I knew what we did, sending a protest letter to the Ghanaian consular general in Hamburg at the time for example. At one occasion too a Ghanaian ambassador was invited to Hamburg to meet the Ghanaian community, the aim being to exchange ideas about how to get Ghana move forward. It was a very emotional meeting; those that were very bitter and angry about how our leaders have betrayed the younger generation were all out to bring it home to the ambassador that they were doing nothing for Ghanaians. One Ghanaian asked the ambassador, with a very angry tone, this question. "Are you free?" It was in the mid 1980s, a period where many Ghanaians were entering Germany and elsewhere in the Diaspora, some with success and others not. At another occasion a Ghanaian Minister came to Hamburg in the 1980s. The Minister asked the Ghanaian student union to arrange a meeting between her, the Minister, and the Ghanaian community in Hamburg. I happened to chair the occasion. It was not easy for the organizers to help tame some of the people in the audience. Many had come there to harm, armed with eggs and so on, the Minster. We, the organizers of the meeting had to vehemently plead with some of the audience to not use violence but dialogue to address any problem facing Ghanaians in Germany and in Ghana. With much effort we succeeded to get the audience to comport themselves.

My encounter with other Africans, as narrated above, has revealed many things that Ghanaians and other Africans in Hamburg during the 1970s and 1980s had in common, many had come to study, to work and to seek protection from political persecution. However, in the pursuit of our individual goals, attitude towards money and how to get it, for example differed among the Africans. The Ghanaian, due to his or her background, had the scope to send things to Ghana by him-herself or through someone in Ghana. It was something one had to do, if one were to be evaluated positively by some fellow Ghanaians, more especially a family member. This brief narration of my encounter with other Africans is meant to help the reader understand why many Ghanaians I met in the Diaspora did what they did. Already in the mid 1980s many 'Old Burgers' (Ghanaians that lived and/or had lived in Germany before) either decided to leave Germany on their own or some were deported back to Ghana. Before I left Germany for good in 1987, after ten years, many Ghanaians I met and knew very well had already left the country for Ghana or for some other countries. What became many of the Ghanaians that willingly or unwillingly left Germany? This is the next issue for our discussion.

5

Leaving Germany Willingly or Unwillingly

Ghanaians Who Left Germany Willingly

As said in this book, there were Ghanaians that pursued studies during the time I lived in Germany and even long before I came to live in the country. Compared with the other groups of Ghanaians, the Ghanaian students in Germany were relatively few. A student that completed his or her studies was required, by law, to return to his or her home country. However, a student would be given some reasonable time, after the completion of the studies to prepare for her or his 'home-going'. The German State even sponsored all foreign students that wanted to undergo some management training (a nine month period) programme before leaving Germany. This was non-obligatory. Many foreign students partook in that training, with some training allowances. A number of Ghanaian students that left Germany, after their studies, had that management training. I, for instance, underwent that training, during which time I got the opportunity to do some practical training at the Daimler Benz Company in Hamburg. Willingly, many other students before my time and after my time in Germany left the country. Some Ghanaian students returned to Ghana to take appointment in some establishments, public or private. Other returnees (students) that assessed that the time was not ripe for them to settle in Ghana made their way for another place (s) in the Diaspora. I, for example, left Ghana in 1987 for Sweden to pursue my Ph.D studies. There were some returnees that stayed to work in Ghana, but were compelled to live after two or four years because of circumstances beyond their control.

It was not uncommon to have met a colleague (a former student fellow at the Hamburg University, for example) who would advise you not to make the same mistake, as he or she did, to return to Ghana, straight after finishing your studies in the Diaspora. This was because Ghana during the mid 1980s was extremely plagued with mass unemployment, scarcity of all the bare necessities of life, high insecurity regarding life and property and massive abuses of human rights. What prevailed was what was termed the culture of silence, where any behaviour or expression that was judged to be in non-compliance of some secrete codes of conduct by the then ruling government, could lead to one's arrest and detention; the worst of it all was that one could disappear in the 'blue'. It was also a period in time when the inflation rate could be as high as 120 percent. The rent for a two or three room apartment could be anybody's guess; it was damned high. Means of transportation was also very expensive (to own a car and use, for example); to travel on the usual 'tro- tro' buses or on taxis was also very expensive. The people were, at the time in question and still, not earning much at all. Food expenditure, medical care expenditure, money for clothes and paying for bills such as electricity and water were really tough for many people. Therefore, those who thought that they were doing a newly arrived graduate from the Diaspora a great service, old colleagues in the Diaspora, own relatives, friends living in Ghana all the years, would advise you to return to the Diaspora and get prepared, before coming to settle in Ghana. Some of the things they would suggest would be as follows: "try to put up a house, (at least for yourself and your core family; because you are expected to house the extended family too) and try to come to Ghana with two vehicles, a private car and a commercial vehicle, for no matter how high one's salary would be it would not suffice; you would need something else to generate extra income. You could imagine how scaring and intimidating the situation was for many students that decided to return to Ghana but did not have the economic backing to live 'in peace and in harmony'. And above all, the atmosphere was such that one could not air his or her grievances about things perceived to be handled wrongly by the government at the time; you would disappear.

It was a period in Ghana when many professionals (e.g. professors, lecturers, medical doctors and nurses) left Ghana for Nigeria, Europe and North America, for example. Some Ghanaian graduates that returned after studies from the Diaspora tried to work in Ghana for a number of years, four or five years, but eventually they could not stand the conditions that faced them. Many that had relations in the Diaspora, through marriage and/or family ties, returned to the Diaspora. Others who did not have family ties in the Diaspora, but could not cope with the unbearable economic and social hardships, managed to make the best out of the situation. Some would pretend as if they were working at their usual place of work (registered as fulltime workers) but would be working elsewhere else as consultants, at the time that they were supposed to be at work; you know what I mean. "If you can't beat them you join them". Many people that worked in the public sector cheated on the government by getting full payment for the whole month, whereas half of their time was used to work for other organisation (s). Many saw these to be 'dirty', but they had no choice. Where again were they going to migrate to? Europe or North America, for instance, has no contractual agreement with Ghana, where workers could migrate freely to both areas.

The message was clear to new graduates that were aspired to return to Ghana, after studies in the Diaspora, to consider going back to complete the unfinished job, "a good preparation before retuning to Ghana to settle down for good". In a country where not only economic and social conditions posed insurmountable problems for many people, but also the political atmosphere and/or the governance structure directly or indirectly encouraged human rights abuses (remember the silence culture in the most part of the 1980s), nobody needed competencies acquired in Europe, North America or elsewhere. Some returnees from the Diaspora, some intellectuals and relatives would even be able to give you names of learned people that have left Ghana. You would be advised to bury your ambitions and visions about coming to help transform Ghana, all to the well-being of the people. Without knowing the contextual variables that would help explain why a group of people or an individual would leave their or his/her motherland, expressions such as "brain drain" and "economic refugees" are used by people without much deeper thoughts about a person's right to live and develop his/her potentialities in peace and in dignity. In spite of all these risks and uncertainties, some graduates that studied in the Diaspora did settle down in Ghana. Those who returned to Ghana but decided to leave again for the Diaspora to accomplish the 'unfinished jobs' still maintained contacts with Ghana through different means, investments and transfers of money to relatives. I will return to this later on. Meanwhile let us also discuss some non-students who also left the Diaspora, (Germany, for example).

From 1983 onwards, if my memory would put me right, the German government issued a policy that sought to win foreigners to accept the state's 're-integration programme'. Foreigners that lived in Germany legally and had worked were given some financial support to return to their respective countries. People that were mostly qualified for the programme in question were those that had legally migrated to Germany, especially after the World War II, to help rebuild the country. To these immigrants were reckoned, for example, the Turks (from Turkey), the Yugoslavs, the Greeks and the Portuguese. Underlying the State's action to support immigrants to return to their countries was, among other things, to be able to meet the problem of unemployment that was increasing among young Germans. I remember very well that in the 1986, when I was doing my Management Training Practical at the Daimler Benz Company in Hamburg, some workers that were 55 years old and above were encouraged to go on pension, making room for the young generation to enter the labour market. Encouraging and/or supporting some foreigners to return to their respective countries were therefore seen as a crucial step to meet the surging unemployment among younger Germans. It was not a compulsory measure, on the contrary. Any foreigner that decided not to return to his or her country was left alone to continue to live in Germany and work. For those that chose to return, the State gave them certain sum of money (a kind of capital) to help them re-integrate in the new society (original country of course). They also had entitlement to their pension and gratuity.

For Ghanaians, no one could be regarded as an immigrant that had originally sought and got immigration status long before he or she came to work in Germany. Almost every Ghanaian at the time acquired the staying and working permits, after one had gone through a number of different procedures such as entering into marriage with a German and having acquired a temporary asylum status with a temporary working permit as a concomitant result. Between 1983 and 1987, when I left Germany, many Ghanaians decided to leave Germany to go and settle in Ghana (their home land). The German authorities extended the 're-integration policy', which enabled foreigners to return to their countries with some financial support to Ghanaians that were returning to Ghana willingly. Thus, a Ghanaian that had worked legally in Germany and decided to return to Ghana, could get his or her pension and/gratuities worked out and paid in cash by the German State. Although many were not up to the pension age, the pension and the gratuities that were paid outright to the Ghanaian returnee was a measure that many Ghanaians appreciated very much and accepted. It enabled many people to return to Ghana with some huge capital in the hand. Even if one did not get the money before leaving Germany, the pension and the gratuity money did reach them no sooner than they returned home.

For many Ghanaians that lived in Germany under constant uncertainty regarding legal staying and working permits, one's legal permits could be withdrawn at any time because the asylum application had been rejected, getting one's pension paid out in cash was a dream that had come into fulfilment. Recall that many Ghanaians had come to Germany, for example, to get some capital and some material wealth, as quickly as possible, and return to Ghana to live a peaceful and economically self-reliant life. Many utilized the 'get your pension money and leave' scheme. They returned, some with containers full of personal effects and some sizable amount of money. I know many Ghanaians that returned to Ghana to begin a new chapter in their lives. Whilst in Ghana, many of the returnees engaged in varied activities, thus invested in several different sectors. Some went into the spare parts industry, importing and selling parts (for the most part second hand parts) in Ghana. Many became 'damned' rich, in terms of Ghanaian standard, that they added the importation of second hand cars too. That was also lucrative. In the course of time, about two thirds of Ghanaians that once lived in German, but had returned to live in Ghana, were engaged in the importing and selling of second hand cars and spare parts.

Many of these spare parts and second hand car dealers were even able to obtain German visa to come to the country and go around themselves to buy and to collect the second hand parts and cars for shipment to Ghana. Many also combined their visits to Germany to buy second hand goods with acting as channels through which some Ghanaians could remit money to their relatives in Ghana. For some of these business people, capital was also raised through those remittances that passed through them. Some business people proved very honest; they sent the money people remitted, through them, to their relatives. There were other business people who proved false. They defrauded people by investing other people's money in their businesses, most of which failed to bear fruits. And if they could not have any positive return on investment, they could not send people's remittances to where they were intended to go. The irony of it was that no business person would tell you that they wanted to borrow money from you, frankly telling you that they were short of capital in Germany, but would pay the money to your mother, a relative or into your bank (because they had plenty of cedis in Ghana) when they returned to Ghana. No business person marketed himself or herself as a person in need of working capital. Almost every one of them created the impression that they were well-to do. The return to Ghana and their engagement in buying and selling second hand goods were lucrative. As many Ghanaians are prone to follow "John", many Ghanaians were enticed into the buying and selling businesses. Already in the 1990s the buying and selling businesses in Ghana had expanded into almost every sector of the economy.

What Ghanaians had known or know, since many years ago, was the buying and selling of second hand clothes. Buying and selling second hand clothes were not so expanded and 'advanced' as it is now. When many Ghanaians returned from the Diaspora, with relatively sizable capital, and went into the buying and selling businesses, Ghana started to witness exponentially a flood of second hand goods of every product category. Second hand cars, trucks, spare parts, second hand white goods (refrigerators and deep freezers, for example), clothes, shoes, electronics, electrical wares and some machinery have become the major areas that many people that returned from the Diaspora have found as their investment fields. The second-hand markets of varied goods attract not only the returnees from the Diaspora, but also many people that live in Ghana. Eventually, the second-hand markets have become very fragmented. One needs to have large volume and/or sales to be able to break even, let alone have some positive returns on investment. Many returnees that I witnessed were doing very well in the second hand markets during the mid 1980s and throughout the most periods in the 1990s, unfortunately had to exit the second hand markets because of bankruptcy and/or difficulty to come by capital that would enable them come to the Diaspora to buy the second hand goods for Ghana. For many, former returnees from Germany, activity in the Ghanaian second hand markets lasted only three or four years. Many had to sell all or most of what they possessed in order to be able to travel again to the Diaspora. A few returned to Germany, while the majority that I knew travelled to North America. I have travelled to Canada and USA, on frequent occasions. I have met many Ghanaians ("ex-Hamburgers") that once lived in Germany. Many of the "ex-Hamburgers", now living in North America, really decided to leave Germany for Ghana to do businesses that would, they hoped, make them travel no more outside Ghana. Some would have this to say, "no matter what one would do and how much one tried in Ghana, the system was/is such that failure would set in. Every body wants to cheat you ("Hamburger")". There are many I have met that say that they do not know what would bring them to go and live in Ghana again. I will return to this issue later on. Let's us briefly discuss others that had to leave Germany against their will; they were deported.

Leaving Germany Unwillingly

As discussed elsewhere in this book there were many Ghanaians that were not lucky enough to secure the legal working and staying permits that would enable them pursue their goals in Germany. They had to live under constant fear and uncertainty, until one day 'the mouse could not escape the cat'. Either they would be arrested, while sleeping at some hide-out apartment, and be deported from there or they would, be arrested because some one had given a tip off to the police. Recall that some fellow Ghanaians could act as informants of the police, reporting their brothers and sister in difficulties to the police. Others were also taken from where they were doing their usual menial work illegally. It was awful to have heard that some one was arrested in some working clothes and, in the working clothes, deported to Ghana. It was not a good scene to have watched a young Ghanaian woman who, upon her arrest, stripped off all her clothes thinking that the police would have mercy on her and leave her alone. That perplexed and inhuman state – the police action and the woman's own reaction – never moved the police and the immigration authorities to reconsider the way some illegal immigrants were apprehended and deported from Germany. There were others that could jump from windows from apartments on fourth or fifth floors of a building, all in the attempt to escape the police raid of illegal immigrants. For some people that had come to live in Germany during the latter part of 1970s and the 1980s, they went through traumatic experiences.

While in hiding some of the illegal immigrants could manage to work for a considerable period of time, say four or five years. But for others, living in Germany was very brief, at most six months. What they all had in common was the risk that they took. They had spent quite some huge amount of money before being able to enter Germany. Unfortunately, their dream to make a better living in Germany turned out to be a nightmare. What should they do? Some decided to face the situation squarely by chasing menial work, one or two or three, so that they could come by money that would be enough for them to return to Ghana or leave Germany for another country with some dignity. Where did such people who were hiding from the police hide their money and/or material gains? Almost every Ghanaian, at the time, had someone in Germany that the former knew at home. Or a relative might have introduced someone ('Old Hamburgers', all Ghanaians) that was believed to have been established in Germany to the 'Ausländer' (A new comer from

Ghana). These relations or acquaintances, for the 'Ausländer' were a major help in that they provided guidance, protection and security for the 'Ausländer'. For instance, the money and some materials that the 'Ausländer' possessed could be given to someone known through such relationships and/or acquaintances. Therefore, in the case of a surprise arrest and deportation, the person, in whom the deportee once entrusted his/her money and property, would be contacted from Ghana to help the deportee. Most of the people that hid from the police had to have someone they could communicate with almost every day. This was deemed very crucial because the person hiding from the police could be arrested and deported anytime.

To cut a long story short, some of the deportees, which had to leave Germany unwillingly, could not cope with the situation they faced in Ghana. They did everything within their might, legal or illegal to return to Germany. It was not uncommon to have had someone that was arrested and deported twice from Germany. Such people were termed as people with bad luck. However, if one ponder over why such people risked much of their lives to travel to a place where they were not needed, the answer would be very obvious. They were running from misery (mass unemployment, absence of some basic necessities of life and above all the disregard for failures). Once you attempted the Diaspora journey, there was no going back with empty hands. People would be teasing or condemning you for having wasted money (especially if you travelled with the help of some family money) and time. It was not uncommon to see that the deportees that had become stranded in Ghana (yes, because they felt they had no place in Ghana and could also not afford to travel again to the Diaspora) would not want to return to their respective villages (most of Ghanaians have rural backgrounds). Some of them joined the urban 'crooks' that engaged in organised crimes such as duping innocent potential travellers who wanted to travel to the Diaspora. They would promise a potential traveller all the legal travel documents to enable one travel to some place in the Diaspora (Germany, England, USA, Canada, and so on) for a fee. They could even lure people to follow them to Nigeria or elsewhere because it was easy to travel from there. About 98 per cent of such empty promises turned out to be a bluff, for which the victims had paid money.

Some innocent ones would even go to the extent of selling all their possessions and follow 'a connection man or woman' to Nigeria, only to be left deeply hurt and disappointed. Why would some people have such an attitude towards money and behaved so cruelly against their fellow Ghanaians who appear to be sitting in the same boat (i.e. facing the same misery) as they are? But not all deportees behaved cruelly towards their fellow country men and women. Some were very decent and had positive attitude towards how to make money, the genuine way.

Some deportees, as said earlier on, could work, while they were in hiding from the police, until they were apprehended one day and deported. The people that helped keep their money and/or material things also lived by their promises and sent all that were the deportees to him or her in Ghana. By that help, some deportees had some sizable capital to do business with. Some went into the buying and selling businesses, selling second hand spares parts, tyres whatever. Others went into other businesses such as running transport for carting cargos; others went into the taxi business. Like many Ghanaians that returned home willingly, these groups of Ghanaians that once lived in Germany worked hard to re-establish themselves in Ghana. Many could even manage to do well- recognised businesses. That enabled them to, after some time, travel to the Diaspora to buy and ship merchandise to Ghana for sale. However, in the course of time, the buying and selling markets became so fragmented that many could not find any profitability in keeping to the business. Some decided to leave Ghana again for the Diaspora, notably not to Germany but somewhere else (e.g. Belgium, Holland, USA and Canada). The buying and selling businesses have done great damage to many entrepreneurial efforts in Ghana, although there are some positive sides too of the phenomenon. I will return to this later on. In the next section I give some accounts of my encounter with Ghanaians and other Africans in Sweden. My strongest interest here is to see whether or not there are similar patterns of attitude towards going to live in the Diaspora to pursue goals, as many Ghanaians and Africans I had contact with in Germany seem to have made me understand, and probably you, the reader, too.

My Encounter with Some Ghanaians and Africans in Sweden

In the latter part of the 1987 I came to pursue my Ph.D studies in Sweden. I came to live in Uppsala, a university city. My first encounter with any foreigners was with people from other countries such as China, USA, Iran, West Germany, and Pakistan. The people I met, from the various countries mentioned above, had all come to pursue some studies at the Uppsala University. We met at students' registration office to report and to register for the various studies, for which we had been admitted. However, we all had the need and expressed the desire to meet each other from there. We exchanged addresses because we were living in different students' hostels. Eventually, it turned out that almost all of us had to, first, do the Swedish language course for foreigners. This brought us again into constant interaction. All that time I had not come across anybody from Ghana. It was at the first week of the start of the Swedish language course that I met a Ghanaian, also having registered to take the same course with us. The Ghanaian became happy in meeting me; I also became glad in meeting my fellow Ghanaian. The two of us and the other foreigners in our language class became good friends, meeting after classes to share experiences and even sharing food. We would be meeting at each other's place in turns. One good year had gone and I had not met any other Ghanaian apart from the

As I Journey Along

one who was in my language class; he had also come to pursue his Ph.D studies, although at a different faculty as mine. Naturally my contacts with the Ghanaian in question developed intensely, meeting each other almost every day after class. We lived at the same students' hostel so we could visit each other unannounced.

The above is an illustration that Ghanaians had not come, in their numbers, to live and to pursue different goals in Uppsala, Sweden, where I lived. The aim of the Ghanaian I met was to primarily study for his Ph.D degree. On one occasion the Ghanaian friend and I decided to attend a social function, which was organized by the Ghana Union in Stockholm, a 45 minute travel with the train from Uppsala. Someone had tipped us that there was a Ghana Union in Stockholm, the capital and the biggest city in Sweden. My friend and I wanted to meet other Ghanaians so we took that chance to visit Stockholm. On arrival at Stockholm, I realized that there was something about the city that reminded me of my experiences in Hamburg, Germany. The city Stockholm is relatively big. There were many foreigners, including Ghanaians, living in the city. Ghanaians, as I know them from my experiences in Germany, like to have some social activities when they are found in large groups as the city Stockholm presented at the time. Any way, we had come to the social function of the Ghana Union, a cultural display to entertain Ghanaians and non-Ghanaians that had gathered. It was late in the evening, from 8.pm (one Friday) to late in the following morning (Saturday). While mingling with the people, the Ghanaians that lived in Stockholm spotted that my friend and I were Ghanaians but did not live in Stockholm. Therefore, almost all the Ghanaians wanted to get to know us and vice versa. Especially the executive of the Ghana Union, whose duty it was to win members and retain them, became very much interested in us and accorded us all the attention that we needed. People 'bombarded' us with drinks, food and information so much so that we remembered the very heritage that all Ghanaians bear with them, the Ghanaian hospitality. We were happy and our host (members of the Ghana Union in Stockholm) too was happy.

As the evening proceeded and people engaged intensely in conversation with each other, especially after some strong drinks had been taken, people started to be a little bit personal to ask about the real intentions for a Ghanaian to in Sweden. Some executive members of the Ghana Union, then, wanted to know from my friend and me what has brought us to live in Sweden? I answered that I had come to Sweden to study; a similar answer was given by my friend. The people who asked us that question started to laugh, something we felt was very impolite but we said nothing. All of a sudden one of them burst to say this: "Here in Stockholm nobody has come to study". He started pointing to some figures by saying that "this guy finished the Kumasi University of Science and Technology, that one finished Legon University and that one was a lecturer there. But here in Stockholm they have all abandoned education. We are here to make money". The other executive members with him nodded in agreement. That was a statement, which I never believed that I was going to hear from people of that calibre, executive members leading groups of Ghanaians in the Diaspora with such a perception. Think about a very young Ghanaian that had come to Europe for the first time, not knowing what is best and how to go about organizing his or her life hearing such an advice. I bet you many would be led astray by people who thought that university graduates abandoning education to run after cleaning and dish washing jobs in the Diaspora was worth the struggle.

Here we were with some 'anti-education' people that tried to convince us, my friend and me, who had come from different countries in Europe to forget about education and go after money. I, for instance had come from Germany and my friend from England, with our respective Masters Degrees to study further for our respective Ph.D studies. They could neither persuade my friend nor me to do as they advised and/or suggested. For me if cleaning offices and/or washing dishes were something I could invest my youthful energy in I would not have left West Germany for Sweden. Of course, a student would not mind washing dishes and cleaning offices, for the sake of making some little money, while studying, but that should not be the student's primary goal for being in Sweden or anywhere in the Diaspora. That unpleasant conversation did not only spoil the rest of the social evening activities for us, it killed the Ghana Union's chance of winning new members. My friend and I never continued to develop and maintain relationship with the Ghana Union in

As I Journey Along

Stockholm. Nonetheless, there were a few Ghanaians that lived and studied seriously in Stockholm; some even earned their Ph.D degrees at the Stockholm University.

On the individual level, I for instance saw no need to waste my time to acquire friends in Stockholm. I became very sceptical about having friends there, for any attempt to forge friendship with some Ghanaians in Stockholm might be a trap; I could easily be driven into the need to expand the base of the friendship once that had been established with one Ghanaian. This is because Ghanaians tend to introduce our friends to other Ghanaians, with whom we get along very well. And in so doing the friendship can also be established between a friend and friend's friends. This is positive if all would have a share of mind that would help us realize our potentialities in a dignified way. Getting along with people that would do all within their might to discourage Ghanaians to get education was a thing I could not compromise with. I therefore decided to keep Ghanaians in Stockholm from a distance. After that unfortunate encounter, I visited Stockholm on a number of occasions. Once, I even did one of my doctoral courses there. If I see someone from Ghana I can, with 90 percent certainty, know that from the facial outlook without having to talk with the person. Very often I met some Ghanaians in Stockholm, while there for a course or for some special purpose. I would greet and even exchange one or two words with the person, but that would be the end of the contact. There was no need for any stable and long-term contacts.

To those that had come to Sweden just to live and to work, there was no such officially agreed upon contract between Ghana and Sweden. Nobody could just migrate from Ghana to Sweden for the purposes of coming to work. How then would someone be able to enter Sweden and enter the labour market? This is where some parallels can be drawn between what many Ghanaians went through in Germany (as discussed above) and what also obtained for many Ghanaians that tried to enter and to work in Sweden, for instance. The alternative ways to secure the needed permits (for staying and for working) were and are (1) entering into marriage or a cohabitation relationship ("Samboförhållande") with a Swedish citizen, (2) applying and obtaining the political asylum status, and (3) have

My Encounter With Some Ghanaians And Africans In Sweden

come to study.

My friend and I belonged to the category three. We had come to Sweden to study so even our respective wives were allowed to join us in the course of time. What I could speculate, I cannot say for sure, was that many of the Ghanaians we met at the day we attended the Ghana Union's social activities, cultural display, could fall into the category 2, trying to secure some political asylum status because there was no way many of them could all be married to some Swedes. As I understood things later on a few of them were genuinely married and had their genuine papers. The bulk of them, especially those that were asylum seekers had it tough like in many areas in Europe. It was not easy for people from Ghana to acquire that status anywhere in Western Europe. Hence, many had to be hiding from the immigration authorities and the police. That forced some of them to use false papers to get their hands on one or two menial jobs in order to make money, for that was the primary goal of many of them for being in the Diaspora. But the fight for illegal immigrants by the Swedish authorities became so intense that many that were living illegally thought it wise to leave Sweden, some for Ghana and some for other parts of Europe or North America. In my travels to other parts of Europe (England and Holland for example) and North America, I have met Ghanaians who once lived in Sweden. I talked to such people, on learning that they had been in Sweden before. I am always curious to know what made them leave Sweden. Many would tell me that it was tough; lack of papers that would give one the right to work, lack of proper and well-paid jobs and the 'cold character' of many Swedes that made them leave Sweden. However, there are other Ghanaians that have lived and pursued their goals in Sweden all these years.

In the city Uppsala, where I lived and studied, the number of Ghanaians increased to about ten families, couples and singles, until I left the city in the mid 1990s. Interestingly, almost all of us were studying. It became easy therefore to have regular contacts with each other because the dominant issue we discussed centred on education and how to complete that. Apart from the children to some families and one or two women that had come to Sweden because of their husbands the rest were all studying at the University of Uppsala. We understood each other's situation so we tried to be sort of supporting and encouraging each other. The social pressure as I witnessed many students giving in to the temptation to abandon education and become business people during my time in Germany was not there among Ghanaians in Uppsala. This is not to say that the pressure to turn one's back to education, even if one has the ability to pursue it, was not prevalent in Sweden too; on the contrary. Recall the story about our encounter with some people at Stockholm who claimed that almost everybody in the city had come there to make just money, not study. This was a clear proof of how group pressure can force someone to conform to some 'conventional wisdom' that steer the lives of the majority of the people one interacts with. At Uppsala, the Ghanaians I met and interacted with on very regular basis did not plunge themselves into some 'buying and selling' businesses that demanded that they abandon education and work to load containers of merchandise that were meant for the Ghanaian market. If one had decided to do that at all, where was he or she going to get the work permit to work and make money? And how would she or he get the staying permit? These were the issues that made us all take our studies seriously and discarded the idea of going after money, no matter what money meant to us. Fortunately for almost all of us, all the Ghanaians I met at Uppsala, the students, could complete their respective studies. Many of us got jobs, in our areas of specialization, immediately after completing our respective studies. I, for example, got a lectureship at a university college after I completed my Ph.D studies. But there were other Africans that I met in Uppsala too. I would try to narrate something about my relationships with some of them.

While in Uppsala I had some friends who had come to live and pursue different goals in Sweden. I had friends from Zaire (now Congo Kinshasa), Eritrea, Ethiopia, Sudan, Kenya, Gambia, Uganda, Nigeria and Tanzania. Some of the friends and I did not have deeper relationships to the extent that we would visit each other at our respective homes. However, we could spend time with each wherever and whenever we met outside our various homes, mostly at the university, at libraries and at shopping malls. For some other friends, we developed strong and close relationships with each other. This development might have partly been explained by the fact that we studied at the same faculty, each pursuing almost similar Ph.D studies with the other friends. Here, my friend from Zaire, my friend from Eritrea and my friend from Kenya were studying at the same faculty; it even came to a point that we shared one office as doctoral students. Our contact with each other, therefore, was daily, especially at the university and in the office. All the same, the friend from Zaire and I, for some 'personal chemistry' were much more close to each other than we were to other Africans. I was interacting more with this friend from Zaire than I was doing with my own fellow countrymen and women in Uppsala. We lived at the same students' hostel so we met almost everyday, sometime at my apartment and other times at his. This close and strong relationship with my friend from Zaire, for example, provided much insight into my curiosity to know some of the primary motives for Zairians to come to live in the Diaspora, for example, Sweden. My friend too was very curios about the driving forces behind the massive migration of Ghanaians into the Diaspora.

The ambition and the attitude for young people from Ghana, as the previous discussions show, had been and still is to come and live at the Diaspora because that seemed to be the only way to escape abject poverty and to be where one can develop his or her potentialities to the full. These behavioural traits among Ghanaians seem to be converging among almost all Africans. My friend and I would be, at times, watching documentary films that featured the conditions under which many young Zairians were facing, as they fought along to make a living in a strange country, France or Belgium, for example. Sometimes the documentary would be on Africans in Italy and elsewhere also. Much of the ordeals, problem with legal staying and working permits, problem of getting skilled and well-paid jobs, problem of getting decent apartment to live in, and the problem of a fellow countryman or woman exploiting his or her own countryman or woman in the foreign land had been a feature that young Africans have been facing over the years, while living in the Diaspora. Yet the trend to help bring other younger relatives to come and alive not only on the periphery, but to also go through hardships goes on unabated among many Africans. My contacts with other Africans, especially those from Zaire, in Uppsala revealed that an African (especially Ghanaians and Zairians as I knew of) has the moral obligation to help bring some relatives to come and live in the Diaspora. You alone could not help solve the insurmountable problems facing your relatives.

Our governments in Africa are not accountable to the people when it comes to the issue of fighting unemployment, lack of houses, combating high inflation, corruption and bribery and the need to guarantee some basic needs for all, irrespective of who you are. Individuals have got to seek solutions to problems such as enumerated above. Hence, there is no wonder that people take to all sorts of practices to make ends meet, even if it would mean like stealing national money to deposit that in foreign banks. Woefully, some head of states do that in Africa, in the face of the massive socio-economic problems facing the country. The former president of Zaire, Mobutu Sesse Sekou (I mentioned his name because he was a public figure, for others, I refrain from mentioning their names), was a classical example. Many cite him as an example of a leader that was richer than that giant country, Zaire, but his riches were deposited in foreign banks. How could he do that? Apart from African countries that were in real internal 'civil wars' (e.g. Sudan and Eritrea before their independence from Ethiopia), many of the Africans that I met had come from countries that ignored providing solutions to the numerous problems that faced their citizens, especially young people. It was, therefore, 'rational', on the part of young people that came to live in the Diaspora, with the hope of improving upon their living conditions. Who wouldn't do that, if conditions at home become unbearable? The White people did that so many years ago. Other races too have, once in their history, moved from some areas of deprivation into others pregnant with all the essentials one needs to survive. It is just that many Africans land in places where, still, they are not given the opportunity to develop their potentialities and, for that matter, realize their goals. As the discussions so far have shown, if one were to look through the 'development ladder' in any European or North American countries, one would find that many people at the bottom of the ladder are Africa immigrants. Evidently, no one can say that all Africans that have come to live and work in the Diaspora are marginalized. Some have succeeded to achieve their goals and are making satisfactory living out of what they have accomplished; but lo, they are very few.

While the struggle to go after money, among younger Africans in Sweden, was a thing for the big city dwellers, Stockholm, Gothenburg and Malmö, Africans that I met in Uppsala were mostly students. My friend from Eritrea, who studied at the same faculty with me, had a lot of contacts with many of his countrymen and women in Uppsala. Many of the Eritrean people had come as refuges so they had the legal status to stay and to work. Through my friend, I was brought to some social functions of the Eritrean people, where I was able to make friends with other Eritrean people. During the time that I was interacting with these people, in the latter part of the 1980s, they were all doing (that was the information I got) what was within their means to support the liberation fighters that were fighting Ethiopia then for their independence. A very encouraging patriotism and/or contribution were the enthusiasm and the tangible support (cash) that they, as told me, sent to the liberation fighters. For example, everyone was morally obliged to pay certain percentage of his or her income towards that course, helping provide resources for the liberation fighters. They were also organizing social gatherings to raise awareness of the problems facing them as a people on the global level. I happened to watch some of the video recordings of some of their global gatherings to raise money, create awareness among the people of the world and to put pressure on Ethiopia to let Eritrea go independent. This was a vivid demonstration of a people that shared a common vision and value. Vision in the sense that they agreed and knew why they wanted to break free from Ethiopia (at least at the time they were fighting). Their common value is in the sense that they might have known why it was worth dying for their freedom from the 'bondage', if you like, of Ethiopia. At last Eritrea gained her independence from Ethiopia. Many people, non-Eritrean and Eritrean, were happy because the bloodshed came to an end. Very impressively, an interim government was put in place to run the country, until a national constitution and a general and a democratic election would be conducted to elect a civilian government. This promise was kept. I, for example, became very impressed, when Eritrea became the first Africa country ever (am I wrong here?), to have allowed its citizen in the Diaspora to go to the polls at some arranged embassies and government premises to cast their votes. If a new country in Africa could do something like this, then, who would doubt that Eritrea would sway from its paths of democracy and power sharing?

By the turn of the millennium Eritrea started to denigrate into the use of undemocratic governance structures and practices that the country seems to be divided now. My friend, for example, who had marketed Eritrea to me and many others that belonged to our network of relationships, started to utter discontent about the way his country was and is being governed. People with different political opinions and whatnots, which are considered by government functionaries as a threat to their positions, can be arrested and imprisoned without trial. State is monopolizing almost all economic activities, although state management is found not to be efficient. Who dare say something against such practices? All this has made my friend and many others, at the Diaspora, become government critics now, writing articles and so on to air their grievances about the way Eritrea is being governed. In recent times (at the time of writing this book, 2005), demonstrations upon demonstrations have been made in Sweden, for example, against the arrest and imprisonment of an Eritrean journalist, who had been living in Sweden, without trial in Eritrea. In Gothenburg, for instance, the demonstrators demanded the immediate release of the Eritrean journalist from prison. Why am I narrating this story about Eritrea's development? I am doing this because it reminds me of what happened in most African countries immediately after the attainment of independence. My country, Ghana, has a historical example of a development that led a sitting president to declare the country as a one-party state, in 1964, after gaining independence in 1957. Why is sharing power difficult for some Africans who mount the political platform as leaders? Instead of mobilizing and encouraging all to help develop our countries, we spend much time and other resources to fight ourselves. Some Eritrean people, including my friend, now cannot freely travel to their country as they used to do immediately after the country attained its independence. I live the story here and take up discus-

My Encounter With Some Ghanaians And Africans In Sweden

sion of my encounter with other Africans in Uppsala.

The other Africans that I interacted with in Uppsala had also come to study. There was a woman Ph.D candidate from Kenya who was my course mate. There was an Ethiopian Ph.D candidate too at our faculty and an Ethiopian that worked as an administrator at our faculty. Alone at my faculty, in the early part of the 1990s, there were six Africans (from Ghana, Kenya, Eritrea, Ethiopia and Zaire). We made a very good team, meeting often to discuss African problems and politics. There was not a single one of us that could cite an example from his or her country about some effective programmes to combat poverty, one of the major contributing factors to the massive migration of young Africans to the Diaspora. Already in the 1960s Indonesia and Malaysia were cited as examples in the third world where governments embarked on balancing regional development and reducing poverty respectively. These countries were directing infrastructure expenditures, especially in transport and irrigation, to rural areas. According to the World Development Report (1990:80), Malaysia's rural poverty, which in 1973 affected 53.3 percent of the population, fell to 19.3 percent by 1989. Within the same time frame as Malaysia's government invested time and other resources to combat poverty, Ghana for example, had changed governments about five times, some through brutal means. The irony of it all was that governments upon governments failed to tackle the poverty issue. In the 20th and 21 century respectively some of the multinational companies that came to Ghana to help develop certain critical infrastructure were the Malaysian Telecom. Analysis such as above dominated our conversations whenever we gathered in our office and/or in some library corridors. We were trying to find when and how our leaders would have the flair to mobilize the people in a committed effort to combat poverty so that Africans, especially the younger generations, would be able to stay at home and find something meaningful to do with their lives instead of coming to be stranded in the Diaspora, as many have experienced. Indeed living in Uppsala was very helpful because almost every one I knew there studied so we had some common grounds for discussions; the craze for money, even if some had that inside them, could not be a topic that anyone would raise at our gatherings. After my

As I Journey Along

Ph.D studies I moved on to other areas in Sweden. I will briefly talk about my encounter with Ghanaians or other Africans at those places too.

In the mid 1990s I came to live and worked at a place called Skövde. I worked as a lecturer at the Skövde University College for eight years, after which I left for another university college, Halmstad University College. Let me narrate a little bit about the Africans I met at Skövde. Strange enough, I did not meet any Ghanaian throughout the whole of my eight years work at the Skövde University. Skövde is relatively small, about 50,000 inhabitants. The largest employer, I am afraid, could be the Skövde University or the Volvo branch factory that produces engines of various kinds. Certainly, these two sources of employment were and are not opened to whosoever is looking for a job; one has got to get some high qualification before being employed by such organizations. There are no other job opportunities such as dish washing at restaurants, cleaning offices and distributing newspapers to households for some fees, opportunities that abound in most large cities. I was not surprised that I did not meet any Ghanaian and many other Africans at this small city. Recall that most of our young Africans prefer to live in the big cities where they could easily get money by doing whatever menial work comes their way. It is not like that at Skövde. However, there were a few Africans I met at Skövde. These were predominantly Somalis and a few Eritrean people. Almost every one of these people was a political refugee. The dreadful circumstances in Somalia (political turmoil) and Eritrea, during the Ethiopia- Eritrean war, bear the responsibility from pushing these young women and men, which I met in this small city, to come and live in a place where most have no chance of ever going to work. Many of them have not the kind of qualification the modern industries and/or universities demand. And there is a keen competition for unskilled jobs these days among many refugees (not only from Africa but also from some parts of the former Eastern Europe, Middle East and Asia) that many Somalis that I met in Skövde were having no jobs. Unfortunately too, only a few could have the ability to study because a lot of them lack basic education from home. What have the leaders of Somalia been doing all these years, after the colonial powers left Africa, for their younger generations? Look at the example cited above about the concerted effort by some Asian countries, especially Malaysia, to combat poverty. You seldom meet someone from Malaysia in the Diaspora who tells you that he or she is a political refugee. Shame unto African leaders who have contributed to bring the untold mental suffering to their young men and women stranded in the Diaspora. Many Somalis or Eritrean people in Skövde may see the situation (unemployment and inability to pursue education or some professional training, for example) facing them as a mental torture, yet there is not much they can do to influence the Swedish system to their favour. Mental suffering that derives from inequality and/or discrimination, in a foreign country, is not uncommon to hear from Africans and even from Swedes who care about the plight of Africans in their country. Discrimination and inequality is a topic I will return to later on. My encounter with some Africans too in Gothenburg, a place I have lived since the latter part of the 1980s until now, need be told.

I have met a very sympathetic and loving Swede, with whom I have a wonderful daughter, so that brought me to officially register and live in Gothenburg, the second largest city in Sweden. While still working at Skövde, living in the small city throughout the working days in the week, I would always come to live with my family during the weekends. And on all public holidays I would be in Gothenburg. In Gothenburg I have met a lot of Africans; almost from every country in Africa there is a representative in Gothenburg. The majority of the Africans I have met come from Somalia. No wonder that they dominate because in recent times their country has been in a total collapse because of the power struggle between various clans and/or war lords. Again young men and women have had to flee their dear Somalia for safety elsewhere. I have made personal friends with some people from Gambia, visiting each other occasionally at home. I have met a number of people from Eritrea, South Africa, Nigeria, Sudan, Uganda and Cape Verde too. However, my contacts with Ghanaians in Gothenburg have been much close and regular. In essence, all the Africans have almost similar reasons for being in Gothenburg, Sweden. I have met well educated Ghanaians who have good jobs in their areas of specialization. I have also met

As I Journey Along

Ghanaians who mainly are here to make money, in spite of the fact that they lack the qualifications that can enable them to get their dream jobs, well-paid jobs. Their option is to take whatever menial work comes their way, something that demands that one does more than one or two jobs to be able to make ends meet. I have also met Ghanaians who are in Gothenburg solely for studies, after which they return to Ghana.

Like the many Ghanaians that I talked about in Hamburg, some of the few Ghanaians I have met in Gothenburg have managed to secure their legal stay in Sweden. Remember that many Ghanaians in Hamburg, in the latter part of the 1970s throughout the 80s and most part of the 1990s, struggled to get political status, marriage status and student status that would enable them to live and work in Germany. Although many did not get the desired political asylum status, for example, they managed to buy time by filing applications and making appeals against negative decisions from the immigration authorities. While some honestly and decently utilized their time to work hard for their money, some took to foul means to come by their money. Some blatantly defrauded their own countrymen and women and also German companies, taking their booties to Ghana to boast to the people there that Germany was a good place for all who would venture the journey to that place. Certainly some of them were making records, in the light of some Ghanaian judgemental pronouncements. For instance, one would hear a statement as this. "This young man or woman went to Germany only three years ago. He/she has been able to put up three houses, one in Kumasi, one in Accra and one in his/her village. He or she has also a big store in Kumasi and a spare parts store in Accra". What signals were some people that defrauded others, engaged in drugs and in prostitution and stealing from companies giving to other able-women and men in Ghana, when the sources of their quick wealth remained unknown to many people? What some people succeeded to inculcate into the minds of many Ghanaians was that there are some treasures lying in wait for hard-working Ghanaians in Germany or in the Diaspora.

Having been confronted with many Ghanaians whose perception of the Diaspora was/is about making money at all costs, some really acquiring their wealth in dishonest ways, I thought I was going to meet similar experiences with the Ghanaians in the big city, Gothenburg. In Gothenburg, I have not heard about any Ghanaian woman or man that has duped his or her fellow countrywoman or man under the pretext of helping the victim by bringing his or her money to some relatives in Ghana or deposit the money in a bank. No story has also been told about someone charging a fellow countrywoman or man to help bring the 'client's' sister or brother to come and live in the Diaspora. Put together, the question I ask myself is. Are not these Ghanaians in Gothenburg also under the social pressure to remit some substantial things home and also to help bring some relatives to the Diaspora? The answer could be anybody's guess. If yes, how are they going about that demand, by defrauding people or dealing in drugs, for example, or they are doing their contributions genuinely? If no, then, what can explain their attitude towards being in the Diaspora and their behaviour while living in the Diaspora? There are about less than100 Ghanaians in Gothenburg. I have come into contacts with many of them, through some organizational activities involving Ghanaians (I will discuss organizing among Ghanaians later on). Majority of the Ghanaians seem to be working, mostly unskilled jobs. A few of them are working in respectable companies and institutions (universities and hospitals).

The few that I have visited privately and vice versa are having responsible jobs at respectable places. Their attitude towards living in the Diaspora and their behaviour are worthy of emulation. They have all studied, at some point in time, to have come to their respective positions in the places that they work. Instead of discouraging other Ghanaians from pursuing education, they seem to cherish the notion that getting some education in the Diaspora would be the best investment any Ghanaian in Gothenburg could make. Some of the Ghanaians I have got along with here in Gothenburg have educated their own children so well that some of the children have university degrees. Compared to some executive members of the Ghana Union that I met in Stockholm during the latter part of the 1980s, the few Ghanaians, with whom I have had close contacts, here in Gothenburg, put education first. Of course, there are other Ghanaians here in Gothenburg who are said to be less interested in education; for them, doing the unskilled jobs for meagre payment seems to be alright. I have not been able to forge so close a contact with Ghanaians that belong to the last category. Nonetheless, they all long to, one day, return to Ghana. Some are held on by a number of factors to accomplish the 'unfinished jobs'. And recall that returning to Ghana demands that one is very well prepared.

Housing problems, ability to foot the costs of education for one's children at the present Ghana (good schools are expensive and can even demand dollars for the fees), the high-dependency ratio that one would be facing, and what to do to earn money, start own business versus being on someone's pay slips, are all issues that need be carefully considered before one can leave the Diaspora for good. These facts and family ties also seem to be a major exit barrier for one to leave the Diaspora, once one has succeeded to make a living in it. I have met friends on a number of occasions and such issues, as above, seem to dominate our conversations. This makes all Ghanaians that I have met very sensitive to, for example, the socio-economic and political developments going on in Ghana. Many have been going to Ghana almost every year, others every second year, all as means to do some feasibility studies and also to invest in some projects that would enable them return home and live within their means. For many, living in the Diaspora has been a rich experience and a proof that one could live within his or her means. But many doubt it, if the same can be said about living in Ghana. Hence, preparing well, before moving finally to Ghana, seems to be the hope and the answer to many people's predicament. But the germane question is when is one going to be able to prepare well? All is not perfect for many that have come from Ghana, for example, to live and work or study in the Diaspora. Some common issues such as discrimination and inequality are discussed very vehemently among almost all Africans that I have come into contacts with in the Diaspora. So even if many Africans, especially many Ghanaians, would want to live permanently in the Diaspora peacefully and pursue their goals, something is not complete for them. My fellow Ghanaians would say "Abonten inte se efie" ('Being outside home is not the same as being at home). Many are sad and bitter at being discriminated at some point in time, but that is a development no one seems to have a control over. One would swallow it when it comes one's way, waiting for the 'redemption day' one day.

7

Having To Put Up with Discrimination and Inequality

It is not a hidden fact that many Africans in the Diaspora would tell you that they have been subjected to some form of discrimination or inequality. A few critical areas would help illuminate this situation that many having been facing. At the search for jobs, under the condition that one is qualified and has the work permit, many would tell you that no matter how many application forms one would send to various companies, even firms that are looking for workers, one would not be called to a single interview. For those who would be lucky to be called for an interview, there is the 99 percent certainty that they would not be taken, especially when competing with a 'native'. For some, they could be considered for a job, if and only if, they would be prepared to take up something, for which he or she is not trained. For others, in spite of their qualifications, the only jobs they can be offered are unskilled ones, cleaning offices and washing dishes. Recall that some young Ghanaian graduates that leave Ghana for England land at the 'cleaning and dish washing industries'. In England, for instance, language could not be so much a barrier for a Ghanaian graduate to be given only cleaning jobs, for example. In Germany or Sweden, some companies would use the language barrier to refuse some Africans good and qualified jobs. Surely, if one is quite new, but has work permit in

Sweden and Germany, for example, it would be difficult for an organization to offer him or her job, if the job demands extensive and intensive contacts with people; the language barrier must be removed first. But is there any justification of Africans that have lived over ten and more years to be refused jobs by using the language argument? Yet, this is the experience many Africans seem to have made; it is sad and it is bitter. "All are not equal in the labour market", many would say.

One glaring example of a discriminatory measure that I personally experienced happened at the time I studied at the Hamburg University, in then Western Germany. I was, like many poor students (Germans and foreigners) dependent on doing some part-time jobs to finance my living in the country. Luckily enough, the German authorities or the University authorities did create a labour office solely for registered university and "Fachhochschüle" students to help us work few hours during a week. Foreigners, while school was in session, had the right to work twenty hours a week to make some money. However, on holidays, a foreign student could work as long as he or she wanted; one's own strength set the limit at which one could work. This was a system that many students used to a great extent. But there was a rule, at which jobs were allotted to students every morning when we reported at the labour office. The rule that prevailed was about taking a queue number, which some bureaucratic officials of the labour office took into their office or kept in their office. Every one would know his or her number because that would be announced through a microphone. The procedure was that the least number, say 1, was the best; and the best number meant that the first job would be given to the person having it, should some companies ring and demanded help from students for a fee. If one had a bigger number one had to wait longer for his or her turn to get a job, when any offer came in. If the system had worked satisfactorily, no one would have had anything to discuss about discrimination and inequality. But it did not work as all had expected. For some time many students were happy because the principle of 'first come, best number' functioned that one might get the available job (s), if one had the first and/or the least number. If a student slept or overslept and came to the labour office at ten o'clock, while others had been there, since six o'clock, the former would reckon with it that he or she would be the last to get a job for the day. This is because being the last on the queue always meant waiting, until others had got job.

For most part in the 1980s, the labour market started to show signs of decline in the search for more hands to work in the factories; firms started to experience decline in demand and/or orders. All the same, they were coming to the university labour office to demand extra help from students. The job opportunities became less and less. This situation, less demand for student labour by firms, produced some negative behaviour in the German authorities that oversaw the process of allotting jobs. No matter how early a foreign student went to the labour office and no matter what good number she/he had, a German that came late and had a high or bad number stood the chance of getting the first job that came to the labour office. Usually all students that visited the university labour office, in search for a job, gathered outside the officials' office, waiting for their number and a job offer to be announced through the microphone. In the course of time, we were hearing announcements such as "a firm needs one or two students to come and work for it, but only Germans (*Nur Deutscher*)". When this qualification, "Nur Deutscher" thing started, it was new to most of us so we did not pay much attention to whether or not it was going to be a permanent phenomenon. Days, weeks and months went by and the new practice, a blatant discrimination and unequal treatment against foreign students had become the norm of the time. Many foreigners realized that it was useless to go to the labour office at all; no matter how early or late one went there, German firms were looking for only German students. Some foreign students, including me, who were so dependent on part-time jobs organized and lodged a complaint with the students' union and even with the officers that were receiving those discriminatory orders and announcing them to do something about that. It was not a good image for a university labour office to be used the way it was being used. Unfortunately, nothing happened to rectify the situation for the good of all, especially foreign students.

But one day something happened to reveal the 'naked discrimination' that emanated from the university office, not from any firm. One day one foreign student wrote down the name of a firm and the job that needed to be done at the firm's factory, but the firm demanded to have only Germans. The student left the office, on writing down the information and looking up the address of the firm, and went to the firm earlier than the German that got the job could come there. The foreign student went to the manager in charge of the workplace and asked if he could do the job. The answer was "why not, that is why I rang the university". The student asked, "Oh, didn't you ask that you wanted only Germans? The manager's answer was "auf gar keinen Fall" (Not at all). The manager was looking for a student that would come to help them, a German or foreign student it did not matter. Could you imagine the reaction of the student and those of us that got the news afterwards? Many foreign students, on hearing that a German firm had denied the claim that they were looking for only German students to come and do part-time work at their factory became very raged and disappointed. Many became disillusioned, therefore, about the role of a university as a channel to facilitate the integration of Germans and foreigners and also demonstrating that it was a place for multicultural interfaces among all people, irrespective of race, colour and background. What was happening then at the public labour office, which was opened to German and non-Germans and students and non-students? The situation there was worst. If you met, for example, ten Ghanaians that were dependent on the public labour office only about two of them would be able to tell you that they got a factory job (s) from the public labour office, on several visits there. The factory work was not only popular, at the time, for any job-seeker, it paid well and workers had unions to protect their interests. Therefore, when many Ghanaians, for example, ended up taking only cleaning and dish washing jobs, with bad pay and no organization of workers, it was not difficult for one to see that development as discriminatory.

Another area of concern is the search for a 'fitting' place to live, rent a room, an apartment and to buy a house. In Sweden, for example, it is not uncommon to find that Africans are concentrated, among other poor immigrants, in housing areas that are deplete with indigenous Swedes. People can point to you that certain areas were full of Swedes but as foreigners started moving in there, the Swedes moved out. This trend is not different in England, Germany, Netherlands, France, Italy, Belgium, Canada and USA. Some Africans that have tried to get apartment from other areas, especially where many indigenous people live, would tell you that it is not without much ado; sometimes you have got to get the backing of an indigenous person before you could be allowed to reside in where you desire. For most Africans, for example, ability to pay rent or buy a house is not a determinant of a place one wants and desires to live in the Diaspora. In my travels to many of the countries mentioned above, friends I have in those areas would show me around, pointing to me, for instance, "who lives where in their common city". Why should things be like that? On the one hand the indigenous people complain that foreigners do not master their language or their codes of behaviour. On the other side, when foreigners want to live near them, mix with them and learn from each other, they move out. The equation is never going to balance then; integration would never come about if we run away from each other. But for an African, for example, it is painful because he or she sees that problem as not being wholly accepted by the indigenous people.

Some foreigners would often use practical experience to illustrate the barriers of entry into the territories of some indigenous people. One would see an announcement about an apartment to let, for example, and one would ring. Here, one's accent would expose him or her. The receiver at the other end could tell you that the apartment is already let out. To find the truth in that information, get an indigenous person to ring, after you, as a way of responding to the room or apartment to let announcement. The answer would be very positive. How does one explain this treatment then, discrimination or inequality? The above discussions tell the reader about some areas where and how discrimination of foreigners does come about. For more such experiences, every African in the Diaspora, for example, might have something to add to the few examples discussed here. For many Ghanaians, for example, the above discussions are contributing factors that drive them to desire to return home (Ghana), for they do not feel 'complete' in a foreign land (s). What efforts or investment are Ghanaians making towards their goal to return to Ghana one day then? I discuss my experience with the efforts some Ghanaians are making in Ghana, channelling their experiences and capital into Ghana. For the dream many Ghanaians in the Diaspora have is that 'being outside home is good, but being at home is best'.

8

Investing In Ghana

Many Ghanaians that I have met in the Diaspora, Germany, Sweden, England and other areas (USA and Canada) left Ghana in their early twenties. Mass migration into the Diaspora among the young people started in the early 1970s. It was a period in time when Ghanaians could travel to many parts in the Diaspora, especially England and West Germany without visas. In the early 1970s many craftspeople such as tailors, taxi drivers and mechanics came to live for a short while in Germany, for example, to do some menial work. Many returned, within a very short time, with some capital or machines to invest in Ghana. Soon such people became recognized and appreciated for their entrepreneurial ventures. These were people who could not have been able to get access to adequate and cheap credit facilities in Ghana, if they had not made the journey to the Diaspora. Many people that returned from the Diaspora, after working to acquire some capital, did not only invest in some businesses, they put up decent houses that differentiated them from those of their neighbours. The returnee from the Diaspora had become self-reliant and was even employing other people. However, this differential advantage that a few enjoyed, during the early 1970s, with capital acquired in the Diaspora and invested in Ghana, produced the effect that many young people wanted to follow suit. Many people tried to travel to the Diaspora, in their numbers, during the later part of the 1970s and throughout the 1980s, many with the goal of making quick money as some had done.

Germany or England, for example, could not absorb many young people from Ghana who were just after getting jobs and making quick money so that they could return home to invest. Already in the mid 1970s, travelling to West Germany or England without visa was abolished. That did not deter many young Ghanaians to travel any-way. Legal or illegal, several people ventured to make the journey. Once they were in the Diaspora many rushed to acquire some capital that would enable them return to Ghana to undertake some invest-ment projects. Some did realize their dreams. But many could not make good use of the capital they acquired in a hard way in the Di-aspora. Many had village background, areas that were denied social amenities such as electricity, good roads, proximity to efficient mar-kets, good drinking water, good health and educational facilities. If a person from a deprived area had made a journey to the Diaspora and on his or her return to Ghana was able to do some recognizable in-vestment in some of the major cities in Ghana, others felt challenged and motivated to make the journey too. Investing in Ghana by the returnees from the Diaspora and those who sent money for people to invest on their behalf all had one major problem, limited markets.

Investment opportunities in the rural areas were limited, although many of the Ghanaians in the Diaspora originated from the rural areas. The people they left in the rural areas still used out-dated techniques in faming; most of them had no access to irrigation sys-tems, high-yielding seeds/crops with short mature life, cheap credit facilities and good roads. The net result was/is that their people, about 70 percent of Ghanaians still live in the rural areas, still had/have low productivity; and so was/is their income. Many Dias-poras could therefore not go back to their villages to invest. Their people had not much purchasing power. It was not possible to live in the village and send goods to the urban areas to sell, if one wanted to do effective and efficient business. All investments had to be made in the major cities. The trend is no different even in recent times.

In the major cities, many business people had to compete fiercely in the limited markets to acquire stores, in which they could sell their merchandise, and to acquire customers and be able to retain them. Going into production was not feasible for many because the cost structure could be so high that one would not be able to com-pete with imported comparable goods or substitute goods. Trade had been liberalised, since 1983, so any kind of consumer good, which

Investing in Ghana

one can think of, is available in the marketplace. Some classical examples of investments that the Diasporas made were in the areas of selling spare parts, second hand cars, second hand clothes, and going into the taxi business. Since many just jumped into businesses without knowing what exactly they had committed resources into doing and how to get where they intended to go, they never reached any meaningful business platform, until they ended up in bankruptcy soon after the start. There were others that went into transport businesses; some had heavy trucks that plied the rural areas to convey commercial goods and cocoa. They could also cart goods to and from the major cities. There were some that went into transporting passengers, in mini buses, from cities to cities or villages to cities. Some invested in hotel businesses and some in running beer bars. The newly Ghanaian investors tended to imitate one another to the extent that a winning formula today became copied and the differential power eroded within a few months, sometimes even weeks. Many also faced harsh economic climate that made it extremely difficult for them to survive.

During the early part of the 1980s, Ghana faced serious economic problems. The state deficit had become very high and its foreign debt grew from US $895 million in 1975 to US $1,429 million in 1979. The International financial institutions decided to disqualify Ghana from receiving further credits (Akwetey, 1994, p. 78). In a desperate attempt to solve the economic problems, the government was using several control mechanisms such as import control, foreign exchange control and price controls. If traders that were heavily relying on imported goods, such as those mentioned above, faced foreign exchange and import controls, one could imagine how many had to struggle to get access, cutting many bureaucratic red tapes, to cheap official foreign exchange and also the permission to import their merchandise; the business climate was dictated by the 'whom you know rules' and not much by efficiency and effectiveness in business. There were not many business people who waged that corruptive fight for cheap and legal foreign exchange; they had to go to the 'black market' to buy expensive foreign exchange. Import controls had the effect, most often, of delaying or depriving some traders from getting some critical inputs not available in the local market. And in business if one's rivals gain some cost advantage over you, because they had access to cheap foreign exchange, you would be out competed. This unfavourable economic climate made many that dreamt to leave Diaspora to go to Ghana to invest lose much of their hard won capital from abroad.

Even during the time that the country was forced by both external and external pressures, because the continuous declining state of the Ghanaian economy brought untold hardship, to undertake economic reforms, economic agents that were not well prepared were phased out of the market. In 1983, the International Monetary Fund (IMF) and the World Bank had come in to help Ghana both financially and also to help reform the country in all aspects, social, economic, political and legal. The Economic Recovery Programme (ERP) that was initiated in 1983 aimed to, primarily, quickly eliminate large state deficit, to correct price and exchange rate distortions (Roe, 1991; Ghana: Handbook of Commerce and Industry, 1988; Asante et al., 2000). In so doing the government embarked upon measures such as general tax increases, a drastic cut in government spending, and subsidies (World Development Report, 1994: 48-49). The foreign exchange rate distortion had to be fixed. Until 1981, for example, Ghana had a fixed exchange rate by which one US $1 exchanged for 2.75 cedis.

The ERP demanded a massive devaluation of the cedi and an introduction of a flexible exchange rate. At the first devaluation attempt, the exchange rate stood $1 = 90 cedis. By September, 1993, one dollar exchanged for 650 cedis (Ghana Drum, September, 1993:30). The domestic interest rate, ranging between 30-35 %, credit ceilings, coupled with the other measures given above, were expected to bring the then three digit inflation, 120 %, down (Roe, 1991; The Ghanaian Chronicle, May 10-16, 1993). The exchange rate had become, all of a sudden, expensive because of the devaluation, cost of borrowing had become expensive and government subsidies had been drastically reduced, in some areas completely removed. These factors combined to present a very tough challenge for traders that had no means to raise capital for importing their goods. The high rate of inflation, credit ceilings and the removal of most subsidies made many potential consumers end up with less purchasing power. The rising cost of doing business, especially where many depended on imported merchandise or production inputs (cost of borrowing was high, devaluation demanded more money for a dollar) could not be passed on to consumers that did not have the purchasing power.

Those that entered the heavy truck industry faced problems such as the increase in the international price of oil and prices of spare parts. Fuel consumption, at exorbitant prices, coupled with high cost of parts due to the massive devaluation of the local currency, made it difficult to service their vehicles. The conditions of Ghanaian roads to and from the rural areas were in bad shape that trucks broke down very often; and when they did break very often, the owners could not foot the expenditure on repairs, replacement of parts and services; and they could not push the high costs of operation on consumers who did not have the purchasing power to accept whatever price level sellers demanded. To be able to buy and ship a heavy truck to Ghana, cliam it from the port and use it commercially required that one had enough working capital, for example. Unfortunately, many did not have enough working capital and found it difficult to borrow money from the bank at interest rates higher than 30 percent. The result was that many had to abandon their businesses. Those who were not quick enough to exit the business had all their hard-won capital dried up. The concomitant result was that some business owners in the truck industry were not only selling their personal effects either to be able to raise money for a second journey to the Diaspora, some began to indulge in the 'passport – visas contracting business', where they started to misguide potential travellers that, with some payments, they could be helped to enter some countries in the Diaspora. The returnee that had gone bankrupt, but failed to accept failure and offer useful advice and/or share experiences with some poor aspiring travellers, would instead sell false information about the treasures in stock for all in the Diaspora. Selling this false information and some physical things such as false traveller's documents and false foreign currencies became a lucrative job for some, while other innocent people suffered by buying such offers. Some people could raise money to pay for the false information and traveller's documents. They would join a plane to some defined destination in the Diaspora. To the woes of some of the deceived travellers, sometimes their false documents were detected by the Immigration Officers right from Ghana and they would be refused to go on board. Some, though with false documents could manage to board a plane in Ghana to travel to their final destination, only to be refused entry. They would be deported back to where they came from. Once I personally travelled with the Ghana Airways from Düsseldorf, via Rome, to Ghana in 1986. The plane made a stop at Rome to take passengers that were bound for Ghana too. At the scheduled time to depart, the Ghana Airways was still in Rome. Several hours elapsed before the passengers on board got to know why we had been delayed. The plane had been delayed because the Italian Immigration Authorities were going to deport some Ghanaians that had entered the country with false papers. One plane brought them to Italy and another plane (this time this Ghana Airways) had to take them back, on the same day to Ghana. You could see the feeling of fear, anger, failure and hopelessness in their faces as they were being escorted to board the plane, back to Ghana. These experiences are worth sharing because lack of enabling environment (for e.g. one in which conditions do not favour businesses to start and be sustained) and living in a society where to fail (after life in the Diaspora, for e.g.) is an ugly thing, have produced the effect that some people would want to survive and succeed at the peril of their fellow man or woman. The Ghanaians that were deported had been helped by some "quack" false passport and visa contractors against fees. One important aspect of the factors that hinder the creation and sustenance of enabling government, bureaucracy, that bear the responsibility for the failures and some 'inhuman' behaviours in some Ghanaians need be discussed.

Bureaucracy: The Post Independence Pathological Development in Ghana

As Bob Marley, the legend of blessed memory, mentioned in one of his famous challenging songs, black people have to emancipate themselves from the mental slavery. This is because no one but the black people themselves can free their minds. Relating this famous lyric to the situation in Ghana, the kind of bureaucracy in Ghana has become a real devastating disease that need be uprooted, before it comes to the stage that the society gets completely destroyed. In the minds of many Ghanaians, it is impossible to get an access to many decision-makers in the public sector without having to go through a dozen of other people (subordinates). And what does going through many subordinates imply? As many Ghanaians may bear me out, going into the offices of some Ghanaian public servants before you get a simple problem solved, the practical manifestation of bureaucracy, would demand that you grease their palms before they serve your need; sometimes it is just about telling where the next officer's office is. There are no hurdles here to be knocked down; you cannot escape some offices and be able to get through with your need or problem. Some under the table payments must be made along the way. This greasing of the palm, popularly known as a corruption in which some government officials indulge, seems to be wholeheartedly accepted as part and parcel of the Ghanaian mentality or culture. Thus, it seems to be a fact that one bureaucrat's activity or resource serves as the input for the next bureaucrat, before a need brought to him or her can be met. Hence there would be no point for you to attempt skidding one bureaucrat, without making some under the table payments, and go to the next. If you do that, the question you would be asked would sound like this: Have you been to the bureaucrat X or Y? If the answer is no, you would be told to start from there. Some of the returnees that started businesses in Ghana but failed with their business, shortly after the start, do tell me that their encounter with the Ghanaian bureaucracy impacted on their businesses negatively.

During the early 1980s into the 1990s, when many returnees started to do businesses, many had to import their goods, which demanded that they obtain, for example import license, register their companies at the Registrar General's Office and buy foreign currencies. When the imported goods arrived at the Ghanaian harbour (s), they had to go through a number of offices to process the claim of their goods; here they would go to a number of custom officers and tax offices and some other ministries, for example. It is the number of offices and the time one would spend by interacting with officers that would force someone to be prepared to do the under the table payments. Otherwise, a claim of goods from the harbour that ought to have taken a matter of hours or at most a day or two can take months, if one was lucky. The inequality that comes into play is that all are not equal when it comes to the enforcement of regulations and rules by some civil servants. If you know some powerful decision-makers personally or you know someone who, in turn, knows a powerful person in some "critical public offices", you would spend no time in getting your needs met. Or if you have the money to pay bribes (greasing palms), you would also have quick service. What is the implication of this pathological bureaucratic practice? To get access to the right person at the right place in good time has become a function of "whom you know", ability to grease palms and having absolute patience and tolerance to accept delays.

If a businessperson's merchandise is delayed at a harbour, because he or she has no money for the greasing of the palm, while his or her rival quickly gets through (e.g. connections with powerful people and greasing of palms) the impact on the person's business could be loss of market share, dissatisfied customers who cannot wait and the danger of having one's goods becoming obsolete (especially for clothing and fashion wares). "If you say you would pay for the various bribes, how you would account for that in your accounts books in a country where we preach accountability?" an ex-businessperson once asked me that question. Bribes are costs. Where in one's accounting books can bribes be taken care of? And can one easily pass on such costs, originating from bribes, to consumers that are faced with an enormous supply of all merchandise? The answer is no. If you do not pay bribes to quickly get your business registered, obtain important import license and clear your goods from the harbour, for example, the opportunity cost of the precious time you spend to go to and from various government offices would be very high to bear. It was no wonder that many returnees that plunged into doing business, but underestimated the absence of the enabling environment, went out of business. Many of them that had returned from the Diaspora to share their experience and capital with the fellow Ghanaians were slapped in the face; "we don't need you".

Investing in Ghana

This pathological disease, bureaucracy, which breads bribery and corruption, does not seem to 'ebb' out even in the recent times where people and their representatives in parliament talk about "no tolerance of bribery and corruption" and preach "transparency". In May 2005, the Minister of Education in Ghana, a former Finance Minister, expressed worries about a publication of Corruption Index study about countries, on a worldwide basis, because Ghana was among the most corrupted societies on the globe. That image, he was afraid, if not washed away would make potential investors, foreign and indigenous, turn away from Ghana. This mental slavery about the acceptance of counter-productive bureaucratic institutions in the Ghanaian society would have to be freed. This would demand transparency, giving guarantees and providing sources where complaints of bureaucratic practices that are counter-productive could be lodged and handled effectively. Without any doubt, there are other areas where many Diasporas have made their mark, regarding their investments made in Ghana, from the money brought from overseas. Even if some attempts that many Ghanaians have been making by bringing capital from the Diaspora to invest in Ghana have not met with success, they have to be commended for the tremendous contributions many have set themselves to make in the country. For most part of the post African history, many African leaders have stolen money from the countries, which they were/are to help develop and sustain. Pathetically, some "leader thieves" returned the money, mostly loans to a whole country, to be deposited into their personal accounts in some banks in the Diaspora.

In view of the above, Ghanaians and also some other Africans that are genuinely trying to bring money, from the Diaspora, to Ghana or other parts of Africa to invest need be officially identified and supported. In 2005, an IMF study revealed that annual total remittances (official ones) to Africa is 32 billion dollars, with the main destinations or recipients being Ghana, Nigeria and Kenya. And as mentioned elsewhere in this book, the recent Kuffour's government in Ghana has officially acknowledged and commended Ghanaians in the Diaspora for contributing about a fourth of the country's total foreign exchange earnings. The remittances, as some experts believe, are becoming the second largest source of foreign direct investment into many recipient countries, including Ghana. But as most of the discussions in this book show, lack of enabling environment, for example, seems to render the massive remittances into Ghana negligible. This brings us to discuss one important area of investment, the housing sector, where many Ghanaians in and from the Diaspora have contributed immensely.

Investment in Housing

Let me cite a typical description of a Ghanaian family in the savannah region as reported in the World Development Report, (1990: 24)

> "In Ghana's savannah region a typical family of seven lives in three one-room huts made of bricks, with earthen floors. They have little furniture and no toilet, electricity, or running water....The family has few possessions, apart from three acres of irrigated land and one cow, and virtually no savings" (p.24)

In Ghana most of the rural people did, and even still do, share a similar situation as the one cited above. Hence, a Ghanaian that has returned from the Diaspora, although with rural background, and wanted to invest in a house, would be forced to put up modern and expensive houses in the urban areas, where access to, for example, pipe-borne water, electricity and educational and medical facilities is possible. A Diaspora who originated from the savannah region of Ghana or from a rural area in Ghana would want to have access to some modern facilities such those mentioned above. This will require that many have to settle in the urban areas, where acquisition of land (a piece of plot) to build on is a major task. Sometimes land or plots had/have to be acquired at exorbitant prices and with much uncertainty. Since many are not from the urban areas, their ancestors own no land there; they have to buy land. In areas like Accra, the capital town, the demand was so high that supply could not match that. Here some unscrupulous land owners, sometimes false ones, took advantage of the Diaspora, who knew very little about who owned what. One plot could be sold to two or three people, all at different prices. It was not uncommon to begin to build on your plot and one day someone stood before you to challenge the ownership of the land. A very embarrassing incident about controversy over building plots in Accra happened in the millennium. An alleged pastor went furious about the fact that someone had built a house, almost completed, on a piece of plot that he, the pastor, claimed belonged to him. The pastor hired someone to use a bulldozer to go and pull the entire building down. One would ask, "How could such an incident happen?" Yes, it did happen because some landowner had sold the same land to two different people. And why did the cheated pastor waited so long for the other buyer to build a house to such a level before he, the pastor, took to such an act of brutality and callousness? That is every one's guess. For me, what was sad about the whole thing is that the victim did not get rage at and punish the fraudulent person, but the other victim; the pastor had forgotten that they were in the same sinking boat (the sinking morals that is hurting the trust between Ghanaians).

The land or plot controversies could resort to protracted court actions, long litigations, and create enmity between Diasporas who ought to have realized their common enemy, the fraudulent Ghanaian, that had set them against each other. When litigation sets in cost of acquiring a land and build a house on it would swell for many. Anyway, many Diasporas managed to handle such unfortunate obstacles that came their way, in their effort to commit resources into building houses. Still dwelling on the citation above, many that wanted to put up houses did not see the rural areas as the next option. One would want to have a house in a place where it would be possible to do business. The market opportunity in the rural areas, as the above citation depicts, was virtually nil. Therefore, many decided to live and build houses in the urban areas.

In the urban areas the poor people outnumber the non-poor. Housing problem has always been a major issue for many people. Hence, the massive investments that the Diasporas started to do in the housing sector was a great contribution, seen from the developmental point of view. In the 1990s the situation of the poor in the urban areas was described as follows:

Investment In Housing

"There is also growing evidence that increasingly only the elite and the wealthy can afford good quality education because it is being priced out of the reach of the poor. Poor parents do not only have to grapple with steeply rising tuition fees, but also the skyrocketing costs of imported school materials.

Cost recovery has been pushed to the extent that most public standpipes in urban areas have been shut down. This has resulted in easy access to water being limited to 'high class' residential areas and the upper income group" (Panford, 1994, pp. 84-85).

As many Ghanaians, Diasporas or returnees from the Diaspora started to invest in the housing sector, they have changed the outlook of many of our urban areas. There are modern houses that have been or are being put up by people all the time, some in areas where no one thought people would invest in buildings there. This is because many areas, now being used as residences of some Diasporas were cut off from the rest of the city by the virtue that there was no road, electricity and water in such areas. As one or two people settle in areas, which are deplete of essential social amenities such as those mentioned above, they would leverage their capabilities and contribute jointly to bring in there electricity and pipe-borne water, for example. Late settlers would draw on the pioneering work of the earlier settlers and be accorded access to the social amenities such as water and electricity. Here, late settlers would be made to make some payment of a fee that would enable them to connect to the electricity or the water brought into the remote area. These types of arrangements and understanding have been the norm and the tradition in many areas in the urban areas, which have newly been occupied by some Ghanaian Diasporas. They have brought a real new face-lift in many of the urban areas in Ghana. People point to the new houses and tell you that they are for the "Burgers" (another way of describing the Ghanaian from the Diaspora). Many have now also started putting up houses in their villages. You go to some rural areas and you will find that the "Burgers" are making their marks there, bringing into the rural areas some modern houses as well.

The rate at which the Ghanaian Diasporas are putting up houses in Ghana impacts positively on other sectors that supply or support the housing sector. As more houses are being built, businesses are generated for cement producers and suppliers, sand producers and suppliers, iron rods suppliers, iron sheets suppliers, wood suppliers, nails suppliers, water supplier and electricity supplier. Craftsmen and women (e.g. bricklayers, carpenters, steal benders, painters, manual workers get businesses. After a building is completed there will be the purchase of some fittings (e.g. louvers, tiles, electrical sockets and gadgets, water closets, sinks, kitchen cabinets, furniture and alarm systems). Taken together, it will be apparent to every one that investing in the housing sector helps fill the cells in the 'input and output' table of a country like Ghana, which are empty. Unlike investments that go into the 'buying and selling' businesses, investments in the housing sector have multiplier effects, looking at the viable employment and/or businesses that are generated in the supplying and/or supporting industries enumerated above. And above all, investment in housing contributes to the tax base of the society. For example, by the erection of a house the owner will constantly pay property tax and other taxes that are regularly collected by the Ministry of Land and the local Stool respectively. The supplying and the supporting industries to the housing sector also do pay income taxes from their earnings. Occupants in completed or semi-completed houses, which are equipped with pipe-borne water, telephone and electricity, would be continually paying regular bills for their consumption of those facilities. All houses, once completed, would need to be maintained and/or service; they also generate jobs and incomes, as the result, for some organisations or people.

However, the housing sector is plagued with some problems that are a threat to the sustainability of the sector in the long run. The sector relies heavily on imported inputs. Building materials such as cement (the local supply is inadequate), iron rods, iron sheets, tools, machines, chemicals (for paints), fittings such as electrical sockets, keys, nails, water closets, pipes, to name but only a few are all imported. The net effect is that the housing sector is very sensitive to variations in factor prices and foreign exchange rate. Although people are buying building materials in Ghana, the ultimate price is calculated in dollars. And when the cedis is falling massively against some hard currencies such as the dollar and the Euro or Pounds, plus rise in factor prices, the final consumer of building materials gets to pay for the surged costs of suppliers of building materials. It is therefore not uncommon to see that some people may take a very long time to be able to complete putting up, say, a three or four bedrooms house. People can abandon a house project, once started, because they lack the capital to let materials flow in, for example. They would return to the project after some months or years have elapsed. Those still living in the Diaspora would have to return to work hard and save towards the completion of their building. Those who have returned from the Diaspora to live in Ghana would suspend the building project, when cost of building becomes high, until such time that some other investments would yield money for the abandoned project. For some people, building a house could be a life-time investment; every bit of your small earnings in Ghana would have to be invested in the building project.

Lack of capacity and the will to promote and support the production of most of the inputs that the building industry relies on, for example, strengthens the preference for the "made in" USA, UK, Japan and Germany's building materials. Building materials and the cost of the professionals that use the materials on one's house are very expensive so you do not expect people to buy any shoddy materials that will not last longer. Building a house in Ghana, the life-span of which can be several years, you would have to heed to the advice of professional sellers and workers by telling you to buy foreign products. The cost of acquisition of materials and the consumption costs of the materials would dictate to you that you have to go for the quality and the expensive ones from well-know countries (here country of origin of materials assumes importance). Unfortunately, many people cannot raise money internally (in Ghana) by, for instance, letting one's other income-generating activities subsidise one's building investment. Many have tried the 'buying and selling' business venture but with no success. It is not less expensive to borrow money from the local banks at interest rates well over 30 percent to put into one's building project. Even if some bank credits can be obtained for that purposes, there is going to be some regular payment of interest before the mature date of the principal amount. Where would the Diaspora, who has no job on his or her own nor employed by someone, be able to pay regular interests and finally the principal amount? All this had made many Diasporas, those having the possibility to return to where they came from, go back to search for additional money for their unfinished project. For some people, travelling down to Ghana often to oversee their housing project would be eating into their financial savings. Plane faire to and from Ghana, carrying along some presents for relatives and friends and carrying along some sizable amount of money and material things for one's own up-keep or use while in Ghana to oversee your project would be extremely expensive.

Regular visits to Ghana would be limited because of lack of money, yet your project must continue, else people would turn the place as their toilet or trash deposit area; very callous and indifferent on the part of those people that are doing that to a Diaspora that is trying to help better the Ghanaian environment. In spite of this problem, you would choose to send money to someone in the family in Ghana or a friend to help finance the project, which has been abandoned by you. Here, too only a few have succeeded to get a trusted person, through whom they can channel their remittances into the project for which they are intended. Some people might help finance, with your own remittances of course, your project but much of the money would end up in their own pocket or in their own projects. If one day you decide to travel, from the Diaspora, to visit relatives in Ghana and also to see how far your project has advanced, you might catch the shock of your life. The project one would be shown might not commensurate with the capital remitted to the person you trusted would help you. I personally and my own personal friends have experienced that, so I know what I am talking about. Some people might never be in Ghana at all when the idea to build a house comes to mind. They may decide, from the onset, that someone in their family at Ghana could very well handle things for them. So the buying of a piece of land or plot, the documentation on the transfer of the ownership of the land, and the beginning of the project by laying the foundation, with some blocks and cements, of the building could all be entrusted into the care of someone in Ghana. Money would be remitted for the project, which has supposedly been started, constantly. The person in charge of the project could even send you some pictures of the work-in progress. That would be a tremendous feeling, seeing that your toils in the Diaspora are bearing fruits, putting up modern and expensive house in Ghana.

Disappointingly, the Diaspora might decide, one day, to travel to Ghana, for a visit and also to see for his -or herself one most important investment he or she is making, only to find that not even a plot has been purchased on his/her behalf. Where did all the money remitted home go to? Where did the pictures on the foundation of the building and what not come from? These scenarios are no jokes; they have happened to some Ghanaians, who meant well to help their country. It is no surprise that many Ghanaians, although many people would give the impression that Ghanaians love each other, have come to realize that many people would want to prosper and meet their whims and caprices at the peril or dismay of their fellowman or woman. We laugh, share meals and volunteer to help each other at some sporadic periods (especially throwing parties), yet real trust is not there. We tend to be suspicious of each other's intentions so opening up for utter co-operation among two or three Ghanaians and even among family members (the last to distrust) is most often very difficult. I have personally, in the name of family, thrown huge amount of money to help some family members that were in need. When it came to their turn to help other members of the same family, the very people that got my help, see no reason why they should use their hard-earned money in the Diaspora to help others. What is making them forget their past, egoism or some hidden hatred against their own relatives or what? As I have been saying all the time, some close friends of mine and even ordinary acquaintances have also added their experiences to mine; revealing how their pioneering sacrifices have been proved nonsense by those that once enjoyed that. Yes, they see helping a relative to be nonsense in the sense that they do not see why they should go to the aid of their needy relatives in Ghana; to hell with them. If they cannot make ends meet, it is their own fault. But in a society like Ghana, a non- social welfare state, where do the masses go for help when they need a roof over the head, food, medical care, clothes and employment, for instance? The government seems to have no solutions to such problems on its political agenda. Hence, the dependence ratio is still extremely high in Ghana. It is not uncommon to have only

As I Journey Along

one person among ten family members that has a job and regular income; morally the bread winner would have many mouths to feed, for example. Relatives in the Diaspora are morally obliged to help those back home. But why should someone that has been helped to leave Ghana and come to live in some affluent and a social-welfare state refuse to help others that are left behind? All in all, the experiences (opportunities and problems) that many Ghanaians in the Diaspora are facing, as they attempt to channel their hard-won capital to Ghana, lead me to also discuss Ghanaians' perception on organization and co-operation.

10

A Ghanaian's Perception on Organization and Co-operation

The discussion on a Ghanaian's perception of organization and co-operation derives from the experiences that I have discussed, so far, from the extensive interaction, which I have had with Ghanaians in the Diaspora. It is a reflection of how I have observed and/or experienced the extent to which Ghanaians see the benefits of getting organized and co-operate in order to achieve individual or common goals. Many Ghanaians in the Diaspora came to live in their respective countries through the hard and the risky way. Foreign embassies or consulates in Ghana will not grant visas to many Ghanaians to travel to their countries. This has for long had serious consequences on many young Ghanaians, physically and mentally. Ever since the latter part of the 1970s many Ghanaians have been risking the journey to Europe, for example, by selling all they possess to acquire false travel documents (mostly the victims would not know the authenticity of the documents) that, they hope, would enable them realize their goal. Many who ventured the journey, through the false means, may not be able to set foot on the 'dream destination' as promised them by the false visa connection people. Evidence abound of many young Ghanaians that were once stranded in countries such as Nigeria, Cote D'Voire, Libya, Egypt and Tunisia, hoping that they could cross to a country in Western Europe and from there to the 'dream destination'. Some could even die along the way, as the result of hunger, thirst, tiredness and depression (mental and physical torments). A government representative in Libya reported in May 2005 of the tragic death of young Ghanaians, as they desperately tried to cross the Sahara desert on bound for Europe. How did they even get to Libya? They might have paid money (to a passport contractor, for it takes a long time to go through the genuine way) to acquire a simple passport and they might have bought a few expensive foreign exchange from all they had saved all their lives. They might have bought a few expensive clothes that befit the journey to the Diaspora. Yet, they never came close to entering their 'dream destination'.

Some Ghanaians may succeed in entering the Diaspora but might not be able to secure their stay. Some could be apprehended, while on the way to do their menial jobs by the police. Others could be reported by their own fellow Ghanaians to the police and would be arrested as the result. Others would be kept into asylum seeking camps for months, being denied access to work or education. These are people that come into the Diaspora illegally and try to find ways to secure their legal stay (those seeking asylum) and also to acquire the legal work permit (some attempt 'paper marriage' and entry into educational institutions). These problems that many Ghanaians have been going through, ever since entry to most countries in the Diaspora, including England (the country that once colonised Ghana), in the mid 1970s, have not sent any signal to Ghanaians that these are national problems, the solutions of which are beyond any single individual. We can all be so individualistic, being as separate as the fingers on one's hand, if the realization of a particular goal is feasible by the efforts of the single individual. However, where individual goal achievement, for instance, is seen to be impossible without the complementary efforts of some significant others, the need to identify, interact and co-operate with others would be crucial. It is not enough for a single person to go to Ghana to warn Ghanaians about the dangers inherent in travelling to the Diaspora at all cost, legal or illegal. Where many add their voices, in a more organized form, to share their experiences with people in Ghana, at several forums (in urban and in rural areas), and with Ghanaians in the Diaspora, Ghanaians could, together with one another, find some less risky and expensive ways to help Ghanaians travel to the Diaspora.

Sometimes it is the people in the Diaspora who would encourage their relatives, spouses and friends to travel to the Diaspora at all cost, legal or illegal; they ignore all the risks and the costs (physical and mental) involved in the uncertain journey that many set themselves to do and send money to push them to 'hell'. Because many Ghanaians have been ending up into going to 'hell', as they fail to enter and secure their stay in the Diaspora. Remember we said earlier on that, once you failed to enter the Diaspora to realize whatever goal you had, returning to Ghana (mostly by deportation) without any visible material things would change your whole being. People would look at you as a failure/looser, some would even scorn you, and others would not accord you the affection and the belongingness, which you once enjoyed among them. You can imagine how relatives would look at you, if you were given borrowed money, for which the family's critical asset' (e.g. cocoa farm) had been pledged as collateral. All this has produced the effect that failure is the last thing a person (deportee, for e.g. from the Diaspora) could live with; he or she would have to fight on again to raise money to try the journey to the Diaspora once more. How do such disappointed Ghanaians, then raise new capital, which will enable them the second or third attempt to enter the Diaspora?

Often times, some people that have failed to enter and work in the Diaspora remain in the urban areas and join the 'false contractors' to search and cheat other potential travellers to the Diaspora, under the pretext that they would help their victims to enter the Diaspora. In the Diaspora, they would promise their victims, a person gets income, even if he or she does not work. Yes, in some countries in the Diaspora you would get some income if you do not work at all. But how does one qualify to be a beneficiary of such a social welfare system? You need to have a genuine legal staying permit that qualifies you to have an access to social money. Not all staying permits (e.g. just students' permit and tourist permit) would enable you to approach a social office for money, when you do not work. The false contractors do not tell their victims all these facts; they lie to their victims about the 'manna' that falls from heaven for all living in the Diaspora. Hence, their victims should get to the Diaspora and all their problems would be over. If in the 21 century about 15 queen mothers in Ghana were deceived by a false contractor that, against high fees, they would be secured visas to England that would enable them to meet Queen Elisabeth II, then, Ghanaians (e.g. in the Diaspora and returnees) owe it as a duty to inform and to educate the people against the opportunities and problems, which the desire to travel to the Diaspora entails.

Within the Diaspora, Ghanaians go through a lot, positive and negative experiences. Discrimination as we discussed above, is less likely to be overcome by a single individual. It would not have the same weight, if a single individual reports to a boss at the workplace, a colleague at the workplace, a friend in one's social network and to some newspaper about the fact that he or she has been subjected to some form of discrimination. The tendency in almost all societies is that numbers have impact. If one particular customer complains that he or she is allergic against a kind of flower placed at the table of the receptionist in a famous restaurant, it is not likely that some measure would be taken to take the flower away. However, if almost all customers that visit the same restaurant complain about the same flower, then, management or even the receptionist would see to remedy the situation. This is because any collective active action of the customers (e.g. boycotting eating there) could have serious consequences for the restaurant. When looking for jobs, apartment, visiting some night clubs and pubs, applying for bank loans and getting promotions at one's workplace are a few examples, which Ghanaians, for instance, would give as areas where they are discriminated at in the Diaspora.

If a Diaspora returns to Ghana, for holidays or for resettlement, there are certain areas where they are also discriminated at. Why, in the world, would a government in power set so high and ridiculous import taxes on personal cars that some Diasporas ship to Ghana, leading to the inability to claim some cars? Sometimes the tax could be even higher than the actual cost of the car. The ultimate result of the discriminatory tax is that the car would be auctioned, after some time, when the owner had not been able to raise money to pay the tax. Strangely enough, the car would be bought, at a cheap auction price, by someone else. The human suffering that such treatment brings on the Diaspora who had bought and shipped a car to Ghana, only to be denied the property can be any one's guess. Before you decide to buy and ship a car to Ghana, there seems to be some information regarding how much tax each car (fulfilling some criteria) would attract so you would prepare for that. However, you would catch the shock of your life, as you would be confronted with different interpretations of the tax system by some customs offices or officers, at the point of claiming your car. At times too self-proclaimed 'revolutionists' in Ghana could single out the Diaspora and take away his or her car from him/her, under the pretext that the car was going to be used for some 'public operations'. Eventually many Diasporas that were subjected to such treatment discovered, to their amazement, that their cars were being used by soldiers in or for private missions. Why did the soldiers not seize, with force, private cars from anybody, a returnee from the Diaspora or someone who had been living in Ghana, but just the Diasporas car? The interface between a Diaspora and some public officers in some other public institutions can also produce strange behaviour; it is not uncommon to experience that meeting one's demand has to be backed by some 'under the table payments' (the corruption that is rampant in Ghana).

A friend (a townsman) had returned to Ghana in the early 1980s, after staying for a number of years in Germany to start a business. He went into the beer bar business. He had to rent an expensive beer bar spot (a big store-like space) in a very 'catchy' area in Accra. To run that business he had to ship down a truck that would enable him to travel to suppliers of different drinks such as beer, liquor, soft drinks, and other accessories from the various producers (in Accra and Kumasi, for example) that were operating at the time. All that would enable him skip the use of middlemen that might add to the cost of operation. When the truck, which was badly needed for my friend's business arrived at the Tema harbour he had to claim it. Not without much ado, because he had to climb several stairs of bureaucrats before hundreds of documents that would enable him to claim the truck were completed, he claimed the truck at last. But just a few metres drive away from the harbour town (Tema) my friend's truck was stopped by some 'busy and angry' soldiers who ordered them (my friend and a driver) to come out of the truck. They obeyed the command and came out of the truck. The next command was that the key of the truck had to be handed over to the soldiers, with their AK47 guns or whatever sophisticated weapons that were, and step aside. My friend, in a humble protest, asked why he should hand over the key of his own personal truck to the soldiers. The answer was as follows. "My friend, if you don't want trouble, do as you are told. We need the truck for some operations." Do you think that private individuals, some of whom were running from ill treatments in Germany, for example, would have used their limited capital to buy expensive assets such as a truck only to be snatched from them by government agents (soldiers) just like that? Why did some Diasporas have to be treated like that? Why would some people in Ghana be indifferent to the sufferings of a Ghanaian returning from the Diaspora?

On hearing that story of my friend, narrated above, I was looking for more evidences of the seizures of cars, trucks and some other material things that were forcefully taken away from some Ghanaian Diasporas. Indeed, I did get information upon information about many Diasporas that suffered as the result of losing some expensive assets because the government in power allowed some of its representatives to treat some Ghanaians inhumanly with impunity. In the longer perspective you ask yourself whether or not such soldiers that pretended that they came to redeem the poor, the masses, were doing what they promised the people. In my view, and probably for many people, some of the soldiers came to enrich themselves at the expense of the poor. Let us consider how my friend managed to get his truck, after some days or weeks, back. He knew an officer (a townsman) in the army so he reported the seizure of his truck, by some soldiers, to him. The army officer, after hearing the report, used his good offices to trace and to re-capture the truck in question from the soldiers and returned it to the owner (my friend). If he knew no army officer that would have meant that he, my friend, would never have had his truck again. Why does all this exploitation, discrimination and inequality go on in the Ghanaian system, especially against the Ghanaian Diaspora, unchecked? In the latter part of the 1970s I personally experienced a shock in my life, when I bought and shipped one deep freezer and one refrigerator from Germany to my relatives in Ghana. I had left some relatives in Ghana, all within an interval of a year from the time I came to Germany and the time I shipped those things, who needed a little bit of a help from me.

Like many of my fellow Ghanaians in the Diaspora, the band between family members and me have been driving me to do the little I could/can to help alleviate their poverty. The little money I had saved from 'dish washing' and 'cleaning' activities, after a year, had to be sent to the family in Ghana. I preferred to send them a "Dormer machine", a metal chain saw meant for cutting wood. None of my relatives was interested in going to the bush to use the machine, on commercial purpose, although some people that possessed similar machines were making money at the time. The choice of my relatives was a deep freezer to be used for selling some soft drinks, 'icekenkey' and ice-water. I did as they suggested and bought not only a deep freezer, but also a refrigerator. When the goods arrived at the harbour a sister and a brother of mine travelled from Kumasi to Tema to claim the items. They were made to go through a number of offices before, after a contact with one of the custom officials, were told that only one of the items could be claimed. What the hell was that? Yes, the government of the time, in 1978, had decreed that if you brought two "white goods" (e.g. refrigerator, deep freezer and vacuum cleaner) the government would take one. Who in his or her right mind, would have bought two items, from one's very limited resources, when he or she knew that only one could be claimed? I had been only a year in Germany, living in a 'Ghetto-like' situation with some other Ghanaians and was doing menial work and was eating lunch, for the most part, while running to catch trains or busses for work. I (one that shipped the items) did not know of such a cruel or ridiculous decree and neither did the shipping agent (through whom I shipped the items from Hamburg) know about the inhuman decree. Why would soldiers make decrees or regulations, which majority of the people would not know anything about but stay in the heads of some custom officers, as this story indicates?

It was not a worthy Ghanaian that the then-government in Ghana robbed in 1978. If regulations and laws governing all aspects of society, including shipping and claiming of items at our harbour were to be transparent and public servants show prompt dealings and dexterity, Ghana would be a better place to live in (for those who live there and those who decide to return to live in Ghana). My sister and my brother had to make a choice among the two items. They chose the deep freezer, of course, because it was two times expensive than the refrigerator. They left the harbour with tears. Later on they reported the matter to a high senior officer (a friend of mine) that worked in the Public Services Commission at the time. He became furious, not only at the treatment given to my relatives at the harbour, but also at the fact that my relatives did not come to him first before going to claim the items. Certainly, if my friend had got to know about the items, he could have helped them to claim the two items without any problem. Do Ghanaians have to, for most of the time, know somebody in a higher position before their demands would be met by some government officials? For my sister and my brother it was too late; they had signed (at the harbour) and given the refrigerator to the government as a present. The question is that did the refrigerator go to the government at all? That was Ghana. And in the 1980s the same treatment, seizing peoples' property (e.g. cars and trucks) at the harbour continued. Today, in the 21 century, it might not be the same, but the ridiculous exorbitant taxes imposed on items from the Diaspora are producing the same effect. Some people are not able to claim their property because of high taxes so they leave them only to be auctioned cheaply for 'second owners'. Yes, they have a saying in Ghana: "we will not travel to the Diaspora but we will be able to buy everything you bring down here". The Diaspora gets cheated, discriminated and slapped in the face for having risked his or her life into the 'wilderness' (life at the Diaspora at the beginning for all is a real wilderness).

If you go to the private sector too, the Diaspora faces some discrimination in Ghana. By your look, people say that anyway, a retailer or a person in Ghana would be able to say that you are living in the Diaspora or have been living in the Diaspora. If you travel by taxi, if you go to buy something from a retailer (especially building materials) and if you hire some labour to do some activities for you, the practice is that they would all try to 'inflate' their prices. They perceive you to be very rich; therefore you are insensitive to higher prices. They would use all tricks to impressive it upon you that you have been treated very well, with very good price (s). Sometimes, while being discriminated by the retailer or the workman, someone else (a third person) would happen to stand close by. After you have completed whatever transaction you have had with your counterpart and have moved some few steps away, the third person that stood by and witnessed how the transaction had evolved and ended would approach you and disclose it that you had been cheated by the counterpart. While exposing the tricks of a fellow competitor to you, he or she would constantly be looking over his or her shoulders to see that the rival does not see or hear the conversation going on between the two of you. The other trader, the one you did not do any business with would ask you this usual question: "Master" or "Brother" or "Sister" "Wo de gyee wo sen?" (How much were you charged for the goods?). You tell the person the prices and she or he would exclaim, "aah, she/he has cheated you. I can see that you are living in the Diaspora ("Burger"). That is why you were made to pay such higher prices. Next time come to my store, if you need similar things. This or that is my store".

The next time you want to buy things you would not even want to go to the market yourself. You would choose to send some relative (a person you trust) to go and do the purchasing for you. Here, too, when accounts are being rendered by the person, after the shopping, other relatives would shout that you have been cheated. This is because someone might have known a place where similar goods could have been bought at relatively cheaper prices. At last, you would not know whom to trust. All this goes to exacerbate the problem, which the Diaspora would be facing in Ghana, by any effort to do something meaningful. Is it sheer poverty that makes fellow Ghanaians treat you differently by, for example, making you pay more taxes, paying higher prices for goods bought and charging more for services consumed? Or is it a mere discrimination (especially when soldiers take away cars from Diasporas with force). This attitude towards the Diaspora and/or behaviour towards the Diaspora in Ghana are not a thing a single individual can change. Some form of organizational action, where many people put their experiences and views together to see how best such problems that face them, both in the Diaspora and their motherland, Ghana, can be solved. All the same, there are some forms of organizational activities among the Ghanaians in the Diaspora, which I have experienced. Let me take that up.

Social Organizations Among Ghanaians in the Diaspora

In all societies there are groupings of people because people have common interests and problems, which they share with each other, when they come together. Without talking about the various classes (upper, middle and lower classes) in societies, people that group together to pursue common interests, exploiting opportunities and/or overcoming problems, which when left to a single individual can be impossible to achieve, do tend to have formal or informal organizations. The various organizational options, formal and informal, enable members in a group to draw on the synergies that members collectively create to enable some goal achievement. To illustrate this, take any group of Ghanaians that come together to accomplish some task, organizing a funeral celebration, a child naming ceremony (an out-dooring), a cultural show, a church harvest or convention, social meetings, public debates and political campaign. In the Diaspora what I have experienced most is the formal organizational gatherings regarding the practising of religion (formal organization), the formation and running of Ghana students' or Ghanaian unions (formal organization) and Ghana-Sweden organization (formal organization) and social clubs (e.g. formal unions along tribal or area lines). The other forms of gathering that show up among Ghanaians (the informal organizations) have to do with some people offering to help someone organize a funeral in honour of a relative that has passed away, helping someone to organize a child naming ceremony and helping to celebrate someone's birthday.

Taking the formal forms of organizations among Ghanaians, I have come into contact with organizations such as Ghana Students'

A Ghanaian's Perception On Organization And Co-operation

Unions, Ghanaian Unions or some Ghanaian unions organized along some 'area lines' (e.g. people from a particular area in Ghana: At-wima, Kwahu and Navrongo, Ashanti and Ga), Ghana-Sweden Part-nership and Ghana-Denmark organization, for example. This gives me the knowledge to discuss many Ghanaians' perception of and understanding of formal organizations. On the one hand, the people would show the enthusiasm and the will to want to form some kind of an organization because, together, they can draw on the members' heterogeneous and complementary resources and activities to achieve both common and individual goals. On the other, many of them do not seem to understand and to commit themselves to the activities and the resources, which each of the members needs to bring into the organization for it to be developed and maintained over time. No organization (a socially-constructed artefact) has some resources of its own and/or acts on its own. It is its representa-tive members that own resources and perform certain activities, all in the name of the organization. Hence members of any organiza-tion, first of all, may have to, for example, define their mission, their goals in the pursuit of their mission, how to achieve their goals (strategies) by specifying in concrete terms what activities to per-form with what resources. It is when some members are confronted with the task to pay some allotted membership dues or fees, to help organize and raise funds and to perform some activities, which will all contribute to some goal achievement, that you find who under-stands what an organization is and what commitment it demands of its members.

Practically, some Ghanaians think that paying lip services that they belong to an organization would be adequate to see resources pouring on its members from some 'invisible' hands. Many would register with an organization and have their names on the member-ship list, but they would never bother to pay their dues or fees or sacrifice to organize some activities that may bring in funds into the organization's coffers. Formal organizations normally have people appointed to hold various offices such as a president, a general sec-retary, a social secretary, information secretary, treasurer, and so on, hoping that each and every one would do his or little task, which when integrated, would provide the holistic solution for the entire organization. The non-executive members are expected to support the officials and, together, also do their utmost best for the growth and retention of satisfied members. People would accept to do as expected of them. But in reality, many would refuse to contribute their respective quotas that guarantee the survival and growth of the organization. Many Ghanaian organizations in the Diaspora, as I have experienced personally and have been told by others in other areas, hardly survive after a year or two. An organization will start with about 15 executive members (those that have pledged themselves to serve) and quite a number of ordinary members but, at most, after a year or two the organization would be left with only four or five executive members and very dormant ordinary members. However, if the few executive members, which remain after others have left, should be able to organize a party, then, many people would show up to participate in the eating, dancing and drinking activities all night. Call them, after a party, for some meeting for discussions of our common interests and problems only a few would respond and/or attend. When a few members that would commit to the running of an organization continuously experience the poor attendance at meetings, lack of commitment of members of the organization and the lack of openness (because people leave the organization unceremoniously) they give up.

For many Ghanaians, punctuality to some scheduled meetings or activities is the last thing they would respect when they see that it is a Ghanaian (s) that is organizing the meeting or the activity. Hence a meeting or a social activity that is supposed to start at, say two o'clock in the afternoon could start at about six o'clock in the evening, if the organizer is lucky. The embarrassing thing is that an organization, with high ambitions, aspirations and engagement, would go to the extent of inviting some important dignitaries such as ambassadors, ministers and mayors to its social function. The dignitaries would arrive on time, but the ordinary member of the organization would be the last to show up.

Why would Ghanaians not show respect for each other, when it comes to honouring invitations and the time set for that? Some would say that it is the African time, which should be applied when a Ghanaian is invited. I say this is 'bush shit'. I am an African but I do not know of this correlation between attitude and behaviour. Yes, the attitude towards a fellow African is that he or she does not bother about time so we can behave anyhow when an African is expecting me at a certain given time. How many Africans would want to tolerate this notion about Africans? Why would not Africans ignore time given them by their white counterparts for a meeting, party or for work? "The white person doesn't play with his or her time", you would hear that from the lips of many Africans whenever they have something to do with a white person. As an example, let me tell you where the Ghanaian can mistakenly ignore even that he or she is dealing with a white person so time is precious. At most of the Ghana-Sweden Partnership meetings and activities, during the time I served as the organization's first president, most of the Ghanaian members mistakenly took the organization to be a purely Ghanaian affair. You would officially invite them to a general meeting at 2 pm, after which there would be a party at 6 pm. Only about four (out of about 40 registered) members plus all the executive members would attend the general meeting at 2 pm. At 6 pm when the party would be supposed to start, only those that attended the general meeting would be present. But late in the evening, from 9 pm onwards, many people would start coming to the party. Sometimes it is at 11 pm that a party would really begin because a large number of people would be present then. At 11 pm. then our Swedish members would be tired and bored by the paucity of the number of members that attended the meeting and even the party so they would leave us. At one of our meetings, one of the Swedish members seized the opportunity to discuss the Ghanaian attitude towards time and the co-operation with non-Ghanaians. He was of the opinion that Ghanaians could waste their own time, but they should not waste other people's time. He meant that once we agreed to meet at a certain time to perform some activities together we should all respect the time, because some people would fulfil that agreement. If we preferred to come so late, that ought to have been made clearer to our white partners so that they would not come to wait for the others, doing practically nothing while waiting. They could have used their time productively somewhere. Many Ghanaians do not think that such disappointments have negative effects on our organizations and human interaction as a whole.

I have had contacts with members of different Ghanaian organizations in Germany, Canada, USA, Australia and Sweden but the problem they all have in common is lack of commitment, openness and having members whose individual interests are placed over and above those of the organization. Yes, organization may have goals, but some individuals may have some hidden goals, which may conflict with the organizational one. And you would never get to know that; they join the organization and leave it unceremoniously. Sometimes those who have quit would not even want to have anything to do with other members again, a behaviour that breeds real distrust among Ghanaians. Throughout the whole of the period (10 years) that I lived in West Germany I was a staunch member of the then Ghana Students' union in Hamburg, serving at one time as its general secretary and at another as its president. I was a founding member and the first president of the Ghana-Sweden Partnership for education and development; I later on came to serve as its vice president. After some time I decided, on some personal grounds, to leave the post of the vice president, but still remained as a member of the organization. All this gives me the knowledge to talk about the way I see the perception, which some Ghanaians have on organizations.

In the area of religion, it is not uncommon to see how some Ghanaians show signs of faithfulness, commitment and dedication to duties to their various denominations. Religion, which can be seen as a system of shared beliefs and rituals, with some moral codes of behaviour among its practising members, seems to attract and retain Ghanaians. In Germany, during one of my recent visits in 2004, I learned that there are about 60 different Ghanaians churches. They meet often for worship and for some social activities. Is it the respect and the fear of the Almighty God that hold them together and to get them to fulfil their promises and/or duties to the course of the church? Or what is that drive and the 100 percent devotedness to a church, by some Ghanaians, attributed to? Why would Ghanaians not transfer the same commitment, trust and devotedness to their

A Ghanaian's Perception On Organization And Co-operation

worldly organizations that are supposedly also meant to help address issues that affect their mental and physical being? Consider the problems discussed above concerning the type of life many face in the Diaspora and back home in Ghana. Ghanaians would have to start to interact, in a more organized way, to help combat poverty, discrimination, injustice, inequality and exploitation wherever they are (in the Diaspora or in Ghana). They should do this collective redress of the vice of the society not only for themselves, but also for posterity. This calls for organizational action.

In some areas, the informal and/or temporal gatherings, Ghanaians can help a friend or a countryman in need to, for example, name a child, celebrate birthdays or celebrate the death of a lost relative. These are all nice and much appreciated, but they have no deeper commitment and continuity. People do not celebrate funerals, for example, all the time, so there would be no incentive to meet and help each other all the time. Even at such occasions (funeral, child naming or birthday parties) there would be no room for discussions on some of the social vices that affect us all. Most of the time people will gather to party or to mourn, anything short of that would be less tolerated. For some of these social activities, some greedy Ghanaians bring their hunger for money there. People would exaggerate the celebration of a child naming ceremony by soliciting for money. Sometimes donating a smaller amount of money at such gatherings could be exposed and the donor humiliated (not directly however). The names and the amount of money given by donors at such gatherings would be mentioned loudly through microphones. People applaud those who donate sizable amount of money; those who donate little would hear giggling like "aaaah so little". It means some people would be embarrassed for not being able to give more. But sometimes not all Ghanaians that attend such social functions would be working at the time; yet they try to donate the little that they might have. If that is not appreciated, the unemployed person might not want to attend any such function, which demands that attendees donate some money. Is that not sad? Unfortunately, such types of informal organizations are very popular among Ghanaians. It is not bad, but much more attention should also be focused on the benefits that can accrue from formal organizations (besides religious ones), where members are expected to, together with each other, discuss societal problems and seek solutions that transcend personal, tribal and political thrusts. One of the serious problems that face Ghana, as many contend, is the issue of brain- drain. We will look at that in the next section.

11

The Brain Drain of Our Time

When a few Ghanaians left Ghana to study in Europe and USA long before Ghana had its independence, there was not much discussions, if any at all, about brain drain. Ghanaians had gone abroad to acquire knowledge that might be of benefit to the country when they returned home after studies abroad. Indeed some of the pioneers that left Ghana to study abroad did return; some of them were the champions of the fight for the independence for Ghana. I do not want to mention names, lest I may forget some of the pioneers that returned from abroad to redeem their country. Undoubtedly, the knowledge and the experiences that they acquired, while they lived and pursued their respective interests in the Diaspora, played a tremendous role in their fight for Ghana's independence. I salute them all.

Immediately after the independence of Ghana, the policy of the government at the time was to actively support and finance many young Ghanaians and even other Africans that called on Ghana for help to go and study abroad. In the mid 1980s I met one Nigeria middle- aged man at the main railway station in Hamburg, Germany. By our encounter with each other, the Nigeria asked, if I was a Ghanaian. My answer was in the affirmative. The Nigerian was on his way to leave Hamburg for abroad, was just waiting for his train, but he asked me to accompany him into a nearby pub for some drinks. I was delighted by that gesture so we went together to a pub. Just before the Nigerian could order drinks for the two of us, he disclosed it to me that he owed Ghana much. He was a well read man, having a very important position either in Nigeria or in England (now I can't remember exactly the country). He felt he owed Ghana because he enjoyed a Ghanaian government's scholarship as he came to study, during the early 1960s, in England. When the man learned that I was also studying in Hamburg, at the University of Hamburg, he was happy for me. But on learning that I was having no scholarship, the Nigerian became very sad and wondered how that was possible. I was not alone in that situation; there were many other Ghanaians and some Africans as well that were struggling just as I was doing. Any way, not to spoil the occasion with my poor condition, I told the Nigerian not to worry about me, for I was able to make ends meet. I was much more interested in knowing whether or not there were several students of his type that did enjoy Ghana government's scholarships in England during the 1960s. And the answer was yes. For me it was positive that Ghana could help many young people to go abroad to pursue knowledge.

It was when several people, that had enjoyed Ghana govern- ment's scholarships, failed to return to Ghana or Africa after their studies that the issue of brain drain became the hot headline in many newspapers and in many public debates. Indeed some people could be in the Diaspora for more than ten or twenty years without visiting Ghana. They would not even remit anything to Ghana either. What made some people fail to return to Ghana or remit relatives in Ghana, after so many years in the Diaspora, could be anybody's guess. Some might have had life really tough that they could hardly fend for themselves in the Diaspora, let alone remitting someone in Ghana. For others, it could be sheer negligence of their moral obli- gation to help Ghana or some relatives left in Ghana. For Ghanaians, this description of the different characters that came to live in the Diaspora immediately after independence is not an unknown phe- nomenon. Some people might have had relatives in the Diaspora in the early 1950s and 1960s that, for some reasons unknown to the relatives, never came back to Ghana on their own. Money had to be sent, from Ghana, to them in the Diaspora before they could buy their plane tickets and ship a few possessions that they might have had. Definitely, people in the Diaspora that became stranded, after studies, and had no rich relatives to help them return home chose to stay and make a living. All in all, the Ghanaian that had been in the Diaspora to study was expected to return home, after studies. If not, he or she might fit into the description of the brain drain syndrome.

In the latter part of the 1960s and the most part of the 1970s, many Ghanaians that were running away from poverty and political harassment headed for Europe and North America (particularly Canada and USA). Many, academicians or craftspeople or unskilled people, were unable to attain a minimal standard of living in Ghana. It was Ghana where equal opportunity for all, at least meeting some basic needs, irrespective of sex, age, education, occupation, physical and mental abilities, was not guaranteed. Instead, corruption and bribery, for example, became the most essential means through which many could get their needs satisfied. One of the brutalised actions in Ghana's history occurred during those period, coups upon coups where even some former heads of states and some statesmen were publicly executed. For most people in Ghana, the brutalism did not improve upon their living conditions either. Hence in Ghana, for the first time in history, ordinary craftspeople (e.g. tailors, seamstresses, petty traders, shoemakers and mechanics), unskilled people (no skills and no education) and the skilled and the educated people migrated in their numbers to Europe, USA and Nigeria, for example. 1983-84, the whole world witnessed the mass deportation of Ghanaians, over a million, from Nigeria. Ghana had failed to improve upon the living conditions of its poor (they have all the time outnumbered the non-poor). There were no measures put in place to satisfy the basic needs of the masses. The successive governments had failed to recognize it that by satisfying the basic needs of the people that could have a positive effect on their productivity. Almost every Ghanaian was and is expected to create his or her own job; this is impossible for many people.

It is only when the little academician leaves Ghana for the Diaspora and has not returned that people start to talk about brain drain. What about the masses (craftspeople, and the unskilled people for example), enumerated above, that continuously leave Ghana and never return? The academician and the other category of people in Ghana are highly interdependent. A shortage of labour in the farms, for example, would affect everybody because short supply of food, for example, would translate into higher prices in an economy where the masses have no regular income. The brain drain of our time should embody also all Ghanaians that have come to live in the Diaspora, but do not want to return or cannot return, for reasons known to them alone. But even here, brain drain should not be used to describe any Ghanaian (a scholar, a craftsperson and unskilled) that is living and working in the Diaspora. How many people have actually taken the trouble to observe and/or to study many returnees that have gone back to the Diaspora because their hard-won capital that was invested Ghana had come to nought? Several returnees that could not get back to the Diaspora have fallen back into the abject poverty, which they once ran away from in search of treasures in the Diaspora. They can no longer make the journey again to the Diaspora because they do not have the means (capital and the legal documents). Returning to Ghana, at all cost, no matter how one would be able to get re-integrated or not, should make many people use the term 'brain drain' very wisely. In the long run, it is about Ghanaians using their resources (tangible and intangible) and experiences to help Ghana and its people, no matter where they find themselves. Ghanaians in particular and all Africans in general pride themselves to have had an African, from the South of the Sahara, to head the United Nations (UN), Busumuru Kofi Annan. Nobody now describes Busumuru Annan as an instrument or a product of a brain drain; he is using his skills, knowledge and experiences to serve all nations, including African countries and Ghana.

Not all Ghanaians might have got the chance to work with the United Nations. And not all Ghanaians or Africans working with the UN would be able to rise to the position of the secretary general. Yet many Ghanaians or Africans that have come to live and work in the Diaspora have been contributing their quota towards the development of mankind, including people in Ghana. The new breed of Ghanaians that have migrated to the Diaspora in the 1970s until today, 21 century, have different orientation and vision, if you like. Many came to the Diaspora with empty hands but they return to Ghana with their hands full of capital to help develop Ghana. It is not uncommon to see some Ghanaians, living and working in the

Diaspora, visiting Ghana almost every year or every second year to undertake some projects. Are they not helping Ghana? Don't they need be commended and encouraged? In some of the preceding sections we have shown that many Ghanaians, for example, would have remained in Ghana to make decent living, if the environment were favourable. Running away from unfavourable environment, instead of making ends meet through bribery and corruption, armed robbery, fraud and lies, should not be a condemnable behaviour. The saying that "if you can't beat them, you join them" should not be entertained. If a returnee would not be able to make any positive impact, in spite of all efforts, he or she should not allow herself/himself to be won into the gangs of corrupt people, for example, and start to bury the good values that she or he has acquired while struggling in the Diaspora. The ordeals that many people go through, while in the Diaspora, could serve as a real catalyst for them to inject into Ghana valuable assets such as capital, dexterity and honesty to build a better Ghana for all living and posterity; for it is only in Ghana that a Ghanaian might feel that he or she is 'complete'.

There are Ghanaians that have been in the Diaspora for over 20 and 30 years or even more. Most of them would proudly say that they have been making their living without any guilty conscience, conscience devoid of bribery, corruption, fraud, deceit and laziness. You approach a number of Ghanaians in the Diaspora and you would find out how hard many of them are working. Some are doing more than one job. If these experiences and the ability to work hard were to be transferred to Ghana by many returnees, the country could be transformed for better. What we probably need in Ghana or Africa may not be sheer capital but the recognition of the fact that external and internal resources are complementary. None of them is a direct substitute for the other. What needs be done is the knowledge to efficiently utilize the combined internal and external resources for the development of Ghana. This is a topic I will finally return to. In modern times, the Ghana government admits that Ghanaians living in the Diaspora, through their remittances, bring in a quarter of the country's foreign exchange. What about some physical investments, houses built, machinery brought to Ghana for investment and so on? Thorough their incessant remittances and visits to do investments of various types, many Africans have shown that they will want to genuinely help develop the continent. Because many of them care and will want to see Africa raise itself from its socio-economic backwardness, they send the little capital that they have earned, through the hard way, not through corruption and bribery, to Africa. But these remittances and capital inflow from Africans are still inadequate, if the internal resources (both human and materials) are not well prepared to take advantage of the external inflow of resources (from Ghanaians and from non-Ghanaians).

When an African or a Ghanaian reads that in 2003, United Kingdom alone gave altogether 5,880 work permits to health and medical personnel from Africa to come to live and work in U.K., the reaction is very strong and bitter. This is because it is Africa that is plagued with serious health problems such as the HIV/AIDS (Acquired Immune Deficiency Syndrome), malaria, diarrhoea and a high rate of child mortality. Hence giving 2,825 work permits to South African health care personnel, 1,510 to Zimbabwean health care personnel, 850 to Nigerian health care personnel and 695 work permits to Ghanaian health care personnel was a big blow to Africa. This treatment from U.K. received great attention in the headline news of major mass media, the biggest brain drain of our time. Medical personnel, as argued above, are not living in isolation in Ghana or elsewhere in Africa. They interact with other people by engaging in exchange relationships, which enable them to satisfy their basic needs. Where the exchange relationships between medical personnel and other members of the society are not creating the values sharable between the exchange partners, no amount of patriotism and the thought to remain in a society where the only means to survive seems to be bribery and corruption, for instance, would let many medical personnel stay on, if they get the chance to travel to where they believe they could make a decent living with no guilty conscience. In Ghana, many have witnessed that many medical personnel, especially those in government hospitals and clinics, find it extremely difficult to serve the people 'clean'. There is the popular saying that in Ghana "if you don't have money and you fall sick, you would die". Many diseases could be cured, if patients were able to pay bribes in government hospitals where the costs are virtually nonexistent or very small. Many who do not have money to do the 'under the table payments' that go into the pockets of some nurses and some doctors, not the government coffers, do die of curable diseases. You could not imagine how some medical personnel would feel when they refuse a patient the care and the service he or she deserves because there has not been any bribe involved. Is this not similar to the treatment other public servants give to some clients that make demands on them, receiving bribes before they approve their licences for them, for example?

Ghana also has foreign medical personnel working in the country. No one would want to speak about brain drain from the countries, from which the foreign medical personnel had come, USA, England, India and Pakistan, for example. This is because the foreign expatriates have come from environments that have done their homework very well. Many medical personnel would not base their motivation to come to work in Ghana on the desire to make money or meet some basic needs. The same cannot be said about our medical personnel. Again, society believes in numbers. Hence, 695 medical personnel leaving Ghana just under a particular year, 2003, became headline news. Some single medical personnel have been, unfortunately, leaving Ghana for Europe or USA through the hard way (some illegal, if you like) so going straight away to practise medicine or nursing work have/had been impossible. Some do land or landed in the "cleaning and dishwashing" industries. Yet, the Ghanaian medical personnel living for abroad, in the modern time, to work is different from some Ghanaians that left the country before Ghana's independence and during the most part of the 1960s. Almost every Ghanaian immigrant into the Diaspora bears the 'family bowl' that has to be filled and shared with all, members of one's own family and the larger community (through the investments many come back to undertake in the country). That is why I speak of the new way to see and to use the phenomenon 'brain drain'. For me, brain drain is a negative terminology in a modern time where young people, deprived of their right to develop their potentialities, take risks to go abroad in search of knowledge, capital and experiences that would help them return to their homeland to do something beneficial for all. My knowledge and experiences, as I journey along

As I Journey Along

in the Diaspora, give me the impression that almost all Ghanaians in the Diaspora or returnees from the Diaspora have a common vision, which need be realized. The vision is about creating a better Ghana for all, irrespective of one's tribe, gender, education, social class and physical or mental abilities. This is a challenge which demands that all and sundry put our heads, physical capital and natural endowments together and help create a better future for all. I therefore end my narrations by providing some thoughts for deliberation by all who care about the future of Ghana and her people.

12

Some Thoughts For Deliberation

The thrust of my narration is to share with all who care about the plight of Africans in general and Ghanaians in particular, especially the younger generation that do not see any hope in meeting their basic needs, if they continue to live in Ghana. Going abroad, especially to Europe or USA, was meant for those that were going to pursue knowledge. There is nothing on records that shows that many Ghanaians that went to study abroad during the 40s, 50s and most part of the 60s had to leave Ghana because of socio-economic hardships that had reduced many to pathetic poor, deprived of the bare necessities of life. The 1970s until today have been the rebellious moment for the majority of the younger people to take their arms (here all that they possess) in the search for places where they could settle and participate in the creation of value, sharable among all. They rebelled in the sense that they never took to physical war with some rulers in Ghana to demand their right to employment, social amenities such as electricity, clean water, good roads, hospitals, schools and protection of life and property; they just took their untapped minds, strengths and motivation away. Anybody who has observed some Ghanaians going about their daily work in the Diaspora will bear me out that Ghana would have gained much by doing all it could to retain such young, energetic and motivated people in Ghana. Today I can assure the reader that there are more than non-professional Ghanaians in the Diaspora than the so called professionals (mostly highly qualified Ghanaians in various fields) in the Diaspora. All Ghanaians (non-professional as well as the professional) in the Diaspora are equally valuable and could/can all be needed in the development of Ghana.

Consider the discussions about why many Ghanaians leave Ghana for the Diaspora to work and the efforts made by many to invest in Ghana, with capital and experiences from the Diaspora. If there were an enabling environment that would facilitate the integration between the external resources (capital, skills, experiences and motivation acquired in the Diaspora) and the local resources (both natural and human), the combined effect of the complementary resources could be amazing. Unfortunately, nothing positive is happening to change the living conditions for many Ghanaians, particularly young people who are unlikely to have the chance to enter into any gainful employment in Ghana throughout the whole of their entire life. Without some purposeful organizational actions and/or programmes to address the interests and problems of young Ghanaians, for example, the net effect of our passiveness and indifference to the plight of the masses, including young medical personnel, could be mass migration into the Diaspora (legal or illegal). Ghana has been experiencing this mass migration of its youthful people since the 1970s; and this trend seems to be going on uninterrupted. The above serves as a point of departure for us to examine some measures or areas that need be taken into consideration to curb the mass migration, to facilitate the integration between external and internal resources and to provide the enabling environment.

The first challenge facing Ghanaians is the ability of our rulers to be self-critical and take direct responsibility for their failures as well as successes. No serious attempts have been made, ever since the 1970s onwards to address the mass migration of Ghanaians (especially young people) into the Diaspora. The political leaders have failed to see that a Ghanaian's perception of the Diaspora and the opportunities that abound there is a major threat to the country's development. Indeed about 80 percent of Ghanaians that make the journey to the Diaspora return home far better (in terms of wealth, however) than most of their comparable fellow Ghanaians that have never been to the Diaspora to work. As Harrison (1993) argues, absolute poverty implies a level of income that imposes real physical suffering on people in hunger, disease and the massacre of innocent children. He sees relative poverty, on the other hand, as the mental suffering that derives from inequality. Undoubtedly, many Ghanaians can be seen as living in abject poverty. Ghana has not been able to address the problems facing many people that live in abject poverty. The uncertain journey to the Diaspora seems to be, for many Ghanaians, the only option left for them to break free from their abject poverty. For some Ghanaians, however, there seems to be the possibility for them to meet their basic needs. Nevertheless, those that are able to attain a minimal standard of living in Ghana also suffer from relative poverty, mental torture that derives from inequality in the society. They see that a comparable fellow Ghanaian, through bribes and corruption, has risen to live an affluent life in the midst of many living under the poverty line. The affluent lives of some people that enrich themselves at the expense of the people are indisputably the yardstick, on which all others are judged when talking about their value and/or position in the Ghanaian society. That is why it is not uncommon to see some well-to-do Ghanaians (in terms of Ghanaian standard of wealth) selling their possessions in order to be able to travel to the Diaspora to search for a far better living standard, according to the belief and the perception of many people.

Private individuals could use their knowledge and experiences of the Diaspora to tell Ghanaians that "all is not gold that glitters". But that is just a drop in the ocean; it has no effect on the hungry Ghanaian. If about 80 percent of Ghanaians that have been in the Diaspora have been able to better their living conditions, the potential traveller to the Diaspora would not believe any individual private testimony about the uncertain situation in the Diaspora. The 1970s and 80s were periods where many Ghanaians in the Diaspora could easily get jobs, mostly menial ones, but the situation changed after the Berlin Wall fell down in the 1990s, for example. The Diaspora, as many perceive, is not raining 'manna' on all that live in it. Africans, since the 1990s, have been competing with many white people from the former Eastern European countries for many menial jobs as well as qualified jobs. Unfortunately, Ghanaians are being out-performed by their rivals in the search for jobs. Job opportunities in many

European countries, for example, have been constantly shrinking since the 1990s into the present time, 21 century. All this affects people who migrate to Europe, for instance, just for economic reasons; the jobs are not there. This trend has also contributed greatly for many countries to restrict migration into their countries. It becomes a great disappointment, though, for many people when they are not able to enter the Diaspora. Without active governmental plan and action to fight abject and relative poverty in the society, many Ghanaians would not give up the 'dreams' to make the journey to the Diaspora because that is the only place they could have a reasonable living standard.

Many rulers in many areas in the Diaspora struggle to combat all those that would want to live in affluence at the peril of many others. Fighting bribery and corruption is a priority for most serious governments; because that undone would set the pace for the injustice and inequality that seem to not only produce abject poverty but also relative poverty. Bribery and corruption are one of the most serious developmental headaches facing Ghana as a country. Ghana's ability to effectively combat abject and relative poverty will depend, in large measure, on increased investment (public and private) and improved social services. The public sector, as some of the preceding sections have shown, is plagued with mismanagement, bribery and corruption. The effect is that resources are not only wasted, they are misplaced, for the most part, because they are not allocated according to some efficiency and effectiveness criteria. He who pays the bribe gets allocation (of resources, contracts and licences, for e.g.). How many people in Ghana do not know of road contractors and building contractors, for instance, who came by their government assignments through the dubious 'under the table payments' criterion? If such anti- developmental practices persist in Ghana, the country would fail to provide its people with employment and some basic social amenities such as good education, good sanitary conditions, better health care, good roads and better communication systems. And when these basic infrastructures are lacking private individual investments, which depend so much on them, would also not yield the expected effects, providing employment, taxes, and inhibiting the migration of Ghanaians to other areas in search of similar opportunities. These are serious problems to be addressed because when job opportunities and basic social amenities are lacking they provide incentives for many Ghanaians, including all professionals, to want to migrate to the Diaspora. Private investors (Ghanaians and non-Ghanaians) would need to invest their resources in an environment where they stand to gain some positive returns on their investments.

Private investments (from Ghanaians and non-Ghanaians) and public investments, in the country's development process, complement each other. It is therefore senseless to allow a few government representatives in areas such as the custom office, Ministry of Industries and Trade, Registrar General's Office and so on to put bureaucratic tapes that hinder swift dealings with private investors. The cost of delay, as the result of filling countless number of documents, visiting a number of officers and, above all, the 'greasing of palms' are all making the cost structure of an investor in Ghana prohibitive, such difficult to account for costs in the accounting books are not easy to be passed on to final customers who already have low income, purchasing power. Some effective measures to combat costly bureaucracy, bribery and corruption would be to do the following: (1) create bribery and corruption teams throughout the country where people can report to when someone feels mistreated because of refusal to pay bribes (2) All processing of documents by public institutions may have time labels, very transparent ones, that tell clients the maximum time to wait for their case to be completed by the institutions. This time frame should not be arbitrary set by the government representatives, but by some focused group (s) who are well vexed in a particular matter. For example, what time it takes to approve of an import licence, a passport application, a visa application, lease application and application for registering a company should be determined objectively by some focused group (s) and this made public in the mass media, internal brochures, and so on. (3) All efforts should be made to reduce the high public-client direct contacts. We should practise the one-spot dealings with clients and government representatives. For example, I send in my application for lease on my piece of land (a property bought) at the Ministry of Land office and that is it. I should be told the time it would take, a very reasonable time, for the application to go through. There should be no fellow up, by climbing various stairs within the Land department and going to Chief's palace to get their part on the application completed. They breed corruption because delay and frustration set in. These should be avoided in modern Ghana where we preach 'zero tolerance to bribery and corruption and waste of time.

The above measures, when adopted, would go a long way to help private individuals and firms to have their problems addressed by effective government institutions. The impact of such prompt dealings and dexterity, for example, would be the boosting of the competitiveness of our local firms, for example, which compete with the mightier imported finished goods. For prompt dealings with firms, for instance, reduce costs, which might be difficult to transfer to customers. In an economy like Ghana only essential goods, offered at competitive prices, could be bought by the customer that has limited purchasing power, many people have very low income in Ghana. And considering the tough competition facing all sellers or producers in Ghana, as the results of trade liberalisation, the flood of imported goods, well designed, packaged and competitively priced, sell better than comparable products made in Ghana. It is therefore not a surprise that many Ghanaian companies, which formerly did actual production in the country, have capitulated to the foreign competition that come in the form of finished goods/services. Ghana Industrial Holding Corporation (GIHOC), Kumasi Jute Factory and now the Juapong Textile Industries and the Ghana Airways Airline, for example, have all collapsed. That is why the 'buying and selling industry' has taken the upper-hand in the exchange of all basic necessities and luxury goods. Ghana stands to gain, if it strives to remove major bottlenecks such as bureaucracy, corruption and unrealistic import duties on production inputs, they all increase costs of doing business. In the long run it is about bringing the costs of doing business in Ghana to some 'acceptable' level, which many investors (Ghanaians and foreigners) would find appropriate. For many Diasporas who might not have anywhere else to invest their capital (they simply want to bring the money from the Diaspora to Ghana), the try, under all odds, to invest in Ghana anyway. But we have seen how many perish a few years after the start up investment.

Some Thoughts For Deliberation

The lack of enabling environment has been one of the major contributing factors for the number of failures that many Diasporas suffered from, as has been discussed elsewhere in this book.

For foreign investors, rulers in Ghana have got to do their utmost best to sell Ghana as an attractive place for investment otherwise they would not come in the expected numbers. This reminds me of a statement, which one World Bank official said about the competitiveness of African countries when it comes to the attraction of foreign investors.

"Private investors will invest where there is the opportunity of profit and, if there were opportunities in Africa, I think they would invest there even if East Germany is also beckoning. What that says to Africa is: 'You have to make yourself attractive and it isn't good enough to be more attractive than the African country next to you – you have to compete with the rest of the world'. And I have to say it, the image of Africa for foreign investors is bad at the present time. It used to be much better in the late '60s. It can be better but there is a long way to go." (West Africa, 16-22 July, 1990: 2114).

The above quotation was a statement issued in the early 1990s about the performance of Africa when considering the continent's effort to attract private investments, which in combination with the public investment, could help influence economic growth, for instance. And as maintained elsewhere, there are strong complementarities among poverty reduction, economic growth and human capital. Combating poverty, for instance, will demand that Ghana actively encourages and supports private investments, showing flexibility, transparency, fairness, providing reasonable tax regimes and reducing bureaucracy summarily, in its dealings with investors. The globalise competition of our time has no place for rulers that are passive, indifferent, visionless and lacking the political will and power to create enabling environment, in which public and private companies and private individuals are able to develop their potentialities to the full. The interdependence among nations in the globalise world has produced the effect that no single country can stop the mobility or migration of its people into other areas, where they perceive that their human capital can best be put to use. This is the problem Ghana has been facing for many years now. I do not think that Ghana has some statistics about how many of its citizens (people of Ghanaian decent) have left the country since the 1970s until now, the 21st century. That statistics could as well provide some knowledge about the reasons why those Ghanaians left the country for the Diaspora; and also hint on whether or not many are prepared to come and settle again in Ghana, finding out why and why not. This is because such statistics might help policy makers to know the driving forces underlying their migration, the positive and negative effects thereof. All this might help address, constructively, the interests and problems of the Ghanaians who now aspire to also make the journey to the Diaspora.

The reason why many Diasporas are not able to return and resettle in Ghana should also be an area that need be study thoroughly. At present it looks as if many Ghanaians in the Diaspora have made some attempts to build houses, yet many do not have the gust to leave the Diaspora to come and settle in Ghana, in their houses. Some Ghanaians have started to give names to houses built by Ghanaians in the Diaspora, which stay empty in Ghana. The houses are called 'ghost houses'. Again, it is a society where people easily find ways to joke or ridicule others without any deeper thoughts about the topic of their mockery. What is preventing one Diaspora from returning to Ghana can be left to go unnoticed, because society believes in numbers, but not when many people are not being able to come down home (Ghana) to enjoy the fruits of their hard labours brought to Ghana from the Diaspora. In this book I have touched, at length, on some reasons why some Ghanaians are not able to get-reintegrated into the Ghanaian society after their stay in the Diaspora. Chapters seven, eight and nine, for example, share some insights on this issue. Not until conditions in Ghana seem to be better, many Ghanaians in the Diaspora do not feel secure to return home (Ghana). But the creation of a better condition in a society is beyond the efforts of a single actor (e.g. the government and business firms). Ghanaians need to have a positive perception of organizational actions and co-operation. Many of the problems facing Ghanaians (those in the Diaspora wanting to return to Ghana) can effectively be tackled when we draw on the synergetic effects of our combined complementary and heterogeneous resources (capital, knowledge, experiences, and contacts abroad and at home). I therefore challenge Ghanaians to form organizations with good people, with shared mind and values. It is only through such collective efforts that many of our problems, which when left to an individual would be impossible to solve, could be effectively addressed. And with a collective voice, we can warn and advise young people in Ghana about the opportunities and the dangers in being in the Diaspora. Where a potential young person or any Ghanaian wants to travel to the Diaspora, in spite of the warnings and advice about opportunities and problems, everything should be done to direct such a person to avoid fallen into the hands of 'false contractors' that might exploit him/or her by giving false information of the treasures in store for all in the Diaspora.

13

You Can Make a Difference

What is preventing one Diaspora from returning to Ghana can be left to go unnoticed, because society believes in numbers, but not when many people are not being able to come down home (Ghana) to enjoy the fruits of their hard labours brought to Ghana from the Diaspora.

There have been some significant world incidents to prove that a single individual can make a difference in an environment that seems to be plagued with man-made conditions, which retard the social, economic, technological and political well-being of the majority of the people in the deprived environment. Mahmata Gandhi (championed the India's non-violent fight for social justice and political freedom in the 1940s) and Dr. Martin Luther King, Jr. (championed the non-violent fight for social, economic and political reforms that could benefit all Americans irrespective of race or colour in the 1960s). These single individuals, very much commended for their contributions towards freedom, justice and prosperity for all, had it extremely tough to make some significant impact on their own people and on the dominant group of people in their respective environment, in their respective efforts to bring some positive changes. In line with the above citation, these individuals had to win several people, those that shared their world views and/or values, on their side, which enabled them to form a collective force that could press home the desired reforms that benefited all, irrespective of who gave birth to a person, the colour and the race of a person. The privileged group(s) in Gandhi's society or King Jr.'s society would not have succumbed to the 'humble demands' (non-violent ones) of these respective individuals, a single person's fight would have gone unnoticed and be fruitless, if some vast majority of people had not teamed up with Gandhi or King.

It was also clear that Gandhi and King had clear cut targets on which their respective demands were made. Gandhi directed his actions to the British colonial rulers because he felt that they were the cause of the socio-economic and political injustices, for example, to which the Indians were subjected. King also felt that Black Americans had, for long, been denied their right to "full citizenship", preventing them to enjoy all the benefits that the Whites in America enjoyed. Hence, many deprived people, in both India and America, could identify themselves with the views and values that both Gandhi and King put forth, as their argument for Independence (in the case of India from the British rulers) and for socio-economic and political reforms (civil rights in the case of America). Yet, it was not easy at all for both Gandhi and King that were fighting to get people who were of "different race" to understand their demands and, hence, to try to get them to meet that. Both Gandhi and King went through many ordeals (suffering from several arrests and physical pains, for example), while they tried to mobilize support and bring their case across to the respective authorities of their respective environments particularly and to the general public the world over. In spite of the massive support and the progress that these heroes made, each of them had to pay a very high price for the freedom, justice and prosperity they demanded for the people, they paid with their own lives. Gandhi was murdered and so was King. What a shame!! Why would the world have to lose men whose crime was nothing but to demand that all men and women be treated equally, no matter who gave birth to you, your colour or race?

Drawing some parallels to what both Gandhi and King accomplished for mankind, during their life time, we find that many countries (especially the so called Third World) are still facing injustices regarding the socio-economic and political problems that are man-made. Why many young men and women migrate, for example, from Africa in general and from Ghana in particular, have been discussed, at some length, in this book. In Ghana, for instance, the people having the political power to bring about reforms, which might, for example, better the socio-economic and political development of the masses are Ghanaians. They are not of entirely different races, which seem to give preferential treatments to their own people. When the British government ruled Gold Coast (Ghana), individuals like the first president of Ghana, the late Dr. Kwame Nkrumah, and others combined their different world views and values to fight for independence from the British rule. The very problems that Ghanaians enumerated to argue for independence from the British rulers are more or less what are driving many young men and women to flock to the Diaspora to seek some individual solutions to their problems. The mass migration of Ghanaians started during the 1970s (I suppose) and that trend is continuous, well into the 21st century. Many individuals that attempted to challenge and demand reforms, from reigning political rulers, landed in political detentions, without trial, and got their economic resources taken away from them, all at some points in time in our post independent history. Others fled into the Diaspora because they could not see any way out of the repressions, mismanagement, discrimination and abject poverty.

Even if individuals are prone to make a difference, in Ghana, the interconnected social and economic relationships between the people prevent them to get some support for their actions. We are dealing with Ghanaians in power and Ghanaians in the civil service that implement government policies. Your world views and values tell you that corruptions are counter-productive so let us fight it. The discriminatory taxes prevalent in the system (some pay more taxes than others for similar goods and services), some rich people getting away with crime (because they can pay people executing justice in the law courts), and the problem of getting your money's worth when dealing with government monopolies (the services of the electricity company and the water corporation, for e.g.) because of poor services are some of the numerous problems that are man-made. They are making life very difficult for many people. Yet, the interconnected social networks among many people suggest that, any of the problems here, when solved, would mean the end of some people's income. Some thrive and make their living on such counter-productive activities. This remind me of a political joke, which many Ghanaians seem to know of. It goes like this:

You Can Make A Difference

Kofi, we hear all what you are saying; they are very good, but we will not take them or adopt them.

The above citation is said to have come from a one time minister of the state when he listened to a fellow Ghanaian, also a one time Prime Minister of the same state, analysing the problems and some solutions thereof to the former. All this means that some people that depend on others for their living may not be prepared to help solve problems that would mean that, for the short time, they might lose their 'easy earned money' (corruption money or allocation of resources that ought to have gone to some proper channel not to them). Negative information about who in the Ghanaian civil service, for example, is receiving bribes, blocking some resource allocations to legible candidates because no 'under-the table payment of fees' has been received, and diverting government resources from projects, for which they were intended, would be difficult to obtain. Many people do cover crime because they think, for the short time, they might not fare well. There is no much long-term thinking among many people who seem to cover crime in our society. But the problem is that how do we get people like Gandhi and King to break through the entrenched attitude of Ghanaians that have it that bribery and corruption are part and parcel of our lives? The phrase: "Obiara baa saa" (No matter who comes to power, it would be the same) is a sign of resignation in many Ghanaians to help solve the numerous problems that are not only driving young and abled people to flee from Ghana, but breeding also diehard criminals. Today Ghana can no longer boast of its friendly people and their hospitality towards foreigners that visit the country. Heavily armed robbers are making life for many people very bitter in the Ghanaian society.

As an individual, start to make a difference, even if many people would find it difficult to emulate your good works and join you to bring a positive change as it happened during and after Gandhi's time in India and King's time in the United States of America. Short-sightedness must give way to long-term thinking, where every individual in Ghana would pledge that Ghana is a place to live in, decently and peacefully. This would demand that you, as an individual, through your examples, would inspire and motivate many others to have common and/or shared interests, which when translated into positive behaviour would help alleviate the pains that many people go through in Ghana today. Every individual must be worried about the conditions prevailing in Ghana now. Ghanaians in the Diaspora, as the present book discusses, seem to be concerned about conditions in their motherland, Ghana. Some have tried, by various means, to help improve upon conditions in Ghana; but for reasons known to many Ghanaians, their efforts seem to have come to no avail. There are still too much cheating, bribery and corruption, discrimination (who gets what critical resources, for example, could be a function of a membership in a political party, whom you know, etc). These practices have worked against any individual efforts to get established, if one is not having "connections" (i.e. knowing people in higher positions) in the society. For most people success in the Ghanaian society will depend upon how one is well-connected to influential people or can pay bribes. Unfortunately, there are some Ghanaians in the Diaspora who might have left Ghana for the simple reason that it was extremely difficult for them to develop their potentialities. Yet, while in the Diaspora, they fail to put their experiences, knowledge and /or skills acquired to help fellow Ghanaians. Instead, some Ghanaians would go to the extent of replicating the exact attitude and behaviour, which they had before living Ghana, by showing greediness and the propensity to exploit fellow Ghanaians.

Until today, some still are charging exorbitant prices by selling, for example, fake travel documents to poor Ghanaians that are running away from poverty and other kinds of hardships; and some also are charging cut-throat prices for helping their fellow Ghanaians to get the legal papers to stay and work in some areas in the Diaspora. Going back to Gandhi and King again, I do not think that their sacrifices to help all get easy and better lives, no matter where in the world they live, would make anybody justify the greediness and the exploitative behaviour of some Ghanaians in the Diaspora. After all, most Ghanaians in the Diaspora do not belong to the well-paid class of workers (they are quite marginalized), yet some Ghanaians, for want of quick and easy money, would take advantage of them and demand huge sums of money from them by helping them to get some legal papers to stay and to work in the Diaspora. It is therefore no surprising that some Ghanaians in the Diaspora do not see anyway out of the problems facing Ghanaians back home in Ghana. For some people, the notion held is that "everyone in Ghana is cheating or is corrupt" so the problems facing Ghanaians seem to be unsolvable. I contend here that this notion is wrong.

Ignorance and lack of trust among many Ghanaians have bred in suspicions and negative attitude towards efforts to jointly or collectively redress social problems among Ghanaians. The time is long overdue for every single individual who sees the need to help make Ghana a better place to live in, and for that matter help all Ghanaians to develop their respective potentialities, to make the active search for people with like minds and shared values. They have to establish contacts with each other, interact regularly (not necessarily face-to-face, but by other means which the information technology accords us in modern times) and in so doing try to create and derive synergies from others. Creating and driving synergies from others, would enable any single individual make some striding impact on the improvement of life in Ghana and among Ghanaians wherever they are. Remember that Gandhi's and King's initiative to help redress the ills of society got the momentum as the result of many people linking their activities (e.g. doing what was expected of them to confirm that they were against all forms of discrimination and injustice) and tying their resources (experiences and knowledge and time, for example) in the fight to eradicate socio-economic and political injustices. Let go the support of corrupt relatives, friends, and political party members. Let go the support of people who exploit others (those pushing their victims into debt and mental pains through fraudulent activities) and let go the support of inhuman laws and regulations that put many citizens into hardships. As said before, society believes in numbers. If a single individual withdraws his/her support to those involved in the vices enumerated above, it would have no impact. However, if many (preferably millions, for Ghanaians are now about 20 million people) people do not support social vices, as mentioned above, and actively work towards their elimination, most of the problems facing Ghanaians at home and in the Diaspora would be solved.

As I Journey Along

Let me end my plea for individual contributions, in the fight to eliminate societal vices and improve upon life for all, by quoting what a statesman (Bill Clinton, ex president of USA) of our contemporary time, drawing on the exemplary work of Martin Luther King, Jr., demanded of his fellow citizens.

> *"Then I put away my notes and gave what many commentators later said was the best speech of my eight years as President, speaking to friends from my heart in the language of our shared heritage:*
>
> *If Martin Luther King were to reappear by my side today and give us a report card on the last twenty five years, what would he say? You did a good job, he would say, voting and electing people who formerly were not electable because of the color of their skin....You did a good job, he would say, letting who have the ability to do so live wherever they want to live, go wherever they want to go in this great country.....He would say you did a good job creating black middle class........in opening opportunity.*
>
> *But, he would say, I did not live and die to see the American family destroyed. I did not live and die to see thirteen-year-old boys get automatic weapons and gun down nine-year olds just for the kick of it. I did not live and die to see young people destroy their own lives with drugs and then build fortunes destroying the lives of others. This is not what I came here to do. I fought for freedom, he would say, but not for the freedom of people to kill each other with reckless abandon, not for the freedom of children to have children and the fathers of the children walk away from them and abandon them as if they don't amount to anything. I fought for people to have the right to work but not to have whole communities and people abandoned. This is not what I lived and died for.*
>
> *I did not fight for the right of black people to murder other black people with reckless abandon.*

So in this pulpit, on this day, let me ask all of you in your heart to say: We will honor the life and the work of Martin Luther King...... Somehow, by God's grace, we will turn this around. We will give these children a future. We will take away their guns and give them books. We will take away their despair and give them hope. We will rebuild the families and the neighbourhoods and the communities. We won't make all the work that has gone on here benefit just a few. We will do it together, by the grace of God". (Clinton, 2005, pp. 123-4)

The leaders and individual citizens of the Third World countries should ponder over the above quotation and help to brighten the corner, wherever they are. With united efforts, as Clinton says, nothing is impossible when it comes to helping all and sundry in a society to live a life worth living as human beings, full of dignity and pride.

Some sources for further reading of some of the issues referred to in this book

Chapter 2

1) For some further information on deterioration of the economic climate, already in the 1960s, see Fieldhouse, D.K., (1978), *"Unilever Overseas" – The Anatomy of a Multinational 1895-1965*, Croom Helm, London.

2) Trade liberalisation, stiff competition and the close down of numerous Ghanaian indigenous firms in the 1980s and 1990s see, for example, Tangari, R., (1992), "The Politics of Government – Business Relations in Ghana: In the Journal of Modern African Studies, 30, 1, pp.97-111

3) On mismanagement in some state enterprises see, for example, *Ghana Exporters' Directory*, (1991), World Wide Press Ltd. Accra

4) For the disincentives and lack of support for Ghanaians farmers see Roe, A. A., (1991), *Economy*: In Regional Survey of the World: Africa South of Sahara (1991), 21st edition, Europa Publications Ltd., (1991), London.; Asante, Y, Gyasi, E.M and Tsikata, G.K., (2000), *Determinants of Foreign Direct Investment in Ghana*, Overseas Development Institute, Portland House, State Place, London – SWIE 5 DP

Chapter 3

For the discussion of the migration of some Ghanaian graduates, including medical personnel, that has been going on for a long time, where majority of them turn out to be labourers or doing menial tasks see, for example, Adjei, M., (1994), Death and Pain, Rawlings' Ghana: The Inside Story, Black Line Publishing Ltd., London.

Chapter 6

That some developing countries have managed to reduce poverty, improved upon the economic and social infrastructures of their rural population, efforts that have reduced mass migration into urban areas in such countries and into the Diaspora, see *World Development Report*, (1990), Poverty, Published for the World Bank, Oxford University Press, Oxford/New York.

Chapter 8

For the serious economic problems that Ghana faced in the 1980s and 1990s see, for example, (1) Akwetey, E., (1994), *Trade Unions and Democratization: A comprehensive study of Zambia and Ghana*, Dissertation, University of Stockholm, Stockholm, (2) *Ghana: Handbook of Commerce and Industry*, (1988/89), Minsitry of Trade and Tourism, Accra, (3) Asante, Y., Gyasi, E.M., and Tsikata, G.K., (2000), *Determinants of foreign Direct Investment in Ghana*, Overseas Development Institute, Portland House, Stage Place, London SWIE 5DP, Ghana Drum, September 1993: 30, *World Development Report* (1994), Infrastructure for Development, published for the World Bank, Oxford University Press, Oxford/New York.

Chapter 9

1) For the living conditions of the rural poor in Ghana see, for example, *World Development Report, (1990),* Poverty, Published for the World Bank, Oxford University Press, Oxford/New York.

2) For the living conditions of the Ghanaian urban poor see, for example Panford, K., (1994), Structural Adjustment, the State and Workers in Ghana: In Africa Development, a *Quarterly Journal of the Council for the development of Social Science Research* (CODERSRIA, DAKAR).

Chapter 12

1) For the discussion of what Africa needs to do in order to attract foreign private investors, which African countries need badly to stimulate growth and create employment, for instance, see *West Africa*, 16-22 July, 1990: 2114

2) For some discussion of absolute and relative poverty facing many people in the Third World see, for example, Harrison, P, (1993), *Inside the Third World – An Anatomy of Poverty*, 3rd edition, Clays Ltd., England.

Chapter 13

For some inspirational and motivational drive to know why and how one can help improve upon lives of people in a society Clinton's book is warmly recommended: Clinton, W.J, (2005), *My Life: The Presidential Years*, Vintage Books, New York.

www.ingramcontent.com/pod-product-compliance
Lightning Source LLC
Chambersburg PA
CBHW020427290526
45785CB00002B/731